Katrina's Legacy:

White Racism and Black Reconstruction in New Orleans and the Gulf Coast

Other books by the author

COMRADE GEORGE: *An Investigation into the Life, Political Thought, and Assassination of George Jackson*

TAKING ON GENERAL MOTORS: *A Case Study of the UAW Campaign to Keep GM Van Nuys Open*

L.A.'S LETHAL AIR: *New Strategies for Policy, Organizing, and Action*

DISPATCHES FROM DURBAN: *Firsthand Commentaries on the World Conference Against Racism and Post-September 11 Movement Strategies*

THE 2004 ELECTIONS: *A Turning Point for the U.S. Left*

Katrina's Legacy:

White Racism and Black Reconstruction in New Orleans and the Gulf Coast

ERIC MANN

Frontlines Press
www.frontlinespress.com

Frontlines Press

3780 Wilshire Blvd. Suite 1200

Los Angeles, CA 90010

(213) 387.2800 info@frontlinespress.com

www.frontlinespress.com

Printed in the United States of America.

Copies of this book can be ordered at www.frontlinespress.com, or contact us directly.

book design: Geoff Ray, cover photo: AP Images

Library of Congress Control Number: 2006931623

Mann, Eric.

Katrina's legacy: white racism and black reconstruction in New Orleans and the Gulf Coast / Eric Mann.

Includes index.

ISBN-10: 0-9721263-2-5

Contents

Acknowledgements

Frontlines Press is a project of the Labor/Community Strategy Center. Our goal is to generate books in direct support of social movements—in this case the heroic and embattled Black people of New Orleans. Through months of writing and editing, we are able to get books out very fast, and bring them to frontline organizers—*Dispatches from Durban* to South Africa for the World Summit on Sustainable Development, and *Katrina's Legacy* to New Orleans as the first anniversary of Katrina, and whole new hurricane season, approaches. So much is needed by so many. Along with funds and coalitional support, which our organization has also provided, books can be weapons in the battle of ideas.

Strategy Center and Bus Riders Union leaders Francisca Porchas, Leigh Waller, Damon Azali, Barbara Lott-Holland, and Mark Anthony Johnson answered the call when help was requested—attending meetings of the Congressional Black Caucus in Washington D.C. on Katrina and national strategy meetings of the People's Hurricane Relief Fund and Oversight Coalition in St. Helena Island, South Carolina, as well as making several trips to New Orleans to help in the community clean-up and rebuild process.

This book is the product of many Strategy Center members who have good editing skills and a willingness to help. Deborah Orosz and Melinda Hurst read earlier and later drafts cover to cover. Palak Shah and Layla Welborn did comphehensive edits at several stages in the project. Dae-Han Song produced the index. Kelly Archbold is developing a distribution plan to get the book to college faculty for course adoptions, to bookstores, community groups, and movement groups in New Orleans, the Gulf Coast, and throughout the country.

The process of write/edit/criticize/re-write/learn/edit seems at times like a never-ending spiral, but at least in theory, it produces a higher level of knowledge and political clarity. I am very appreciative of how comrades were willing to hang on every word—even if changing many of them in the process.

Frontlines Press is, in the final analysis, the product of the work, leadership, and dedication of designer/editor/producer Geoff Ray and senior editor Lian Hurst Mann.

Geoff takes the final drafts and magically, over many long days and nights, turns type and paper into a fully designed book. Lian helped to shape the politics of *Katrina's Legacy* from the beginning, as we had an urgent conversation about New Orleans, the Black Belt South, and our historical obligation to act in the first days of Katrina. Almost a year later, she spent weeks reading, editing, and researching 12 to 15 hours a day to get the final draft out the door.

Finally, my gratitude to the work of W.E.B. Du Bois, Harry Haywood, Malcolm X, Amiri Baraka, and Komozi Woodard, whose living words shaped so many of the ideas in this book and in whose political tradition *Katrina's Legacy* is situated.

Author's Introduction

There are times in history—slavery, mass lynchings, the Black-led urban rebellions throughout the United States during the 1960s, the Black-led urban rebellion in Los Angeles in 1992, and Hurricane Katrina in August/September 2005—when manifestations of the crisis of Black people in the U.S. require national and worldwide attention and aid. *Katrina's Legacy* is a tactic to challenge the ideology of white supremacy that shapes national policy. It is an effort, in that ideas are a material force, to provide political and ideological support to the struggle for democratic rights and self-determination of Black people in New Orleans, the Gulf Coast, the Black Belt South, and throughout the U.S.

I first became involved in the Civil Rights Movement in 1964, when students from North Carolina A&T State University (an historically Black college) who had risked their lives to simply sit in at a lunch counter asked students at Cornell University to join the "civil rights revolution." Shortly thereafter, I went to work with the Congress of

Racial Equality (CORE) in Harlem and the Northeast, and I have been "a soldier in the army" ever since.

At the height of the "two decades of the sixties,"[1] the Black Liberation Movement at home and the growing independence movements for self-determination in Asia, Africa, and Latin America shaped my antiracist, anti-imperialist perspective. My view, then and now, is that *it will take a worldwide, anti-imperialist united front to isolate and weaken the U.S. government to win self-determination, ecological sanity, and an end to poverty, racism, and war in the world.*

Inside the United States, the key to that strategy is a multi-class Black United Front. In turn, that Black United Front is key to the strategic alliance inside the United States between the multiracial, multinational U.S. working class, led by the oppressed nationality working class, and the oppressed nationality Black, Latino, Asian/Pacific Islander, and Indigenous peoples. In turn, this strategic alliance inside the U.S. is part of a worldwide united front against imperialism as a system led by the oppressed nations and peoples of the Third World.

At this moment in history, the nascent forces of resistance must meet the challenges created by the New Orleans catastrophe and the crimes and punishments of the Bush Administration, the Democratic Party and the capitalist system as a whole—often reflected in the persistent and seemingly never-ending hatred toward Black people in this country by the majority of the white population. And yet, there stands before us a great historical opportunity to help jump-start a renewed Black Reconstruction in the U.S., as part of the project to rebuild the U.S. Left and to reconstruct an international antiracist, anti-imperialist united front to confront the U.S. empire.

The present painful historical period offers an opportunity and an obligation to resist. The Bush Administration is on the defensive and facing greater isolation in the world. The forces of Black resistance have been weakened by decades of repression, division, and disorientation—conditions experienced by all sectors of the U.S. Left. But Black people in New Orleans and the South are fighting to come up with new programmatic initiatives, demands, and forms of organization out of the struggle for survival of an entire people and, from there, to reach out to form a multiracial alliance. *Katrina's Legacy: White Racism and Black Reconstruction in New Orleans and the Gulf Coast* is an effort to contribute to the debate about the central question facing all of us in the movement: Where do we go from here?

Katrina's Legacy began as an internal paper to the leaders of the Labor/Community Strategy Center and Bus Riders Union in Los Angeles. Now, with the encouragement of comrades in the Gulf Coast, it has become a public discussion paper to generate constructive and engaged debates about movement strategy and tactics.

Right now, the People's Hurricane Relief Fund and Oversight Coalition and a broad coalition of grassroots groups are generating tactical plans and demands for federal reconstruction under community control. Saladin Muhammad of Black Workers for Justice has also written an important strategic paper, "Hurricane Katrina: The

Black Nation's 9/11!"[2] Their ideas are presented in the pages that follow.

Many of the ideas presented here are rooted in the scholarship and polemics of W.E.B. Du Bois, Malcolm X, Randall Robinson, Amiri Baraka, and other Black strategists whose work is referenced throughout this discussion. They are also based on lessons from the theory and practice of my own organizational affiliations and alliances that I have participated in from 1964 to the present—Congress of Racial Equality (CORE), Student Nonviolent Coordinating Committee (SNCC), Newark Community Union Project (NCUP), Students for a Democratic Society (SDS), Black Panther Party, Attica Prisoners Support, August Twenty-Ninth Movement (ATM), League of Revolutionary Struggle (LRS), United Auto Workers (UAW) Local 645, the Bus Riders Union, and the Labor/Community Strategy Center.

The central objective of Katrina's Legacy is to reinforce the historical perspective, rooted in centuries of struggle by the Black Liberation Movement, of four interrelated strategic demands—land, Reparations, full democratic rights, and the right of self-determination, up to and including the right of secession from the United States. This conditional relationship of Black people and a Black Nation is in sharp disagreement with the point of view that tries to liquidate the struggle for Black self-determination, and which tries to explain and restrain the events in New Orleans and the Gulf Coast as "attacks on the poor" or "the working class," and which aggressively denies the existence of a Black Nation in the Black Belt South and throughout the U.S. Although of course a focus on class is essential, in the actual history of the United States, as an oppressor nation that oppresses whole nations and peoples inside and outside its borders, *the central "class" question is the national question*, that is, the fight for full democratic rights, for self-determination, and for independence of those nations and peoples oppressed by the United States. Inside the United States, we can only understand class consciousness and class unity by how much workers and peoples of different nationalities work together for the liberation of the oppressed nationalities, and how much the white sectors of the working class work to fight white supremacy and free the colonies, and in this case, fight for Black liberation.

The system's structural, ideological, cultural, economic, and governmental racism has inflicted its attacks on all classes inside the Black community, and thus has created the material basis for a multi-class Black United Front. It is the historically determined Black/white contradiction particular to the U.S. that sets the context and shapes the paths of resistance of all oppressed nationality movements and all strategic thinking upon which to rebuild a U.S. Left.

The present period, shaped by the ongoing disintegration of urban centers, as reflected in government attacks on the Black community in New Orleans, intensifies the challenges to build an explicitly pro-Black, pro-people of color, pro-Third World ideology and movement that combats the white supremacy and "great nation" chauvinism of this country (too often reflected in the U.S. Left), and challenges the system itself.

Katrina's Legacy supports a movement for a Black Reconstruction, a Third Reconstruction in U.S. history, based on the belief that Black people in the U.S. have the right to self-determination, including an independent land base in the Black Belt South, new forms of state unity to consolidate Black voting blocs in the South and urban centers throughout the U.S., political independence from the repressive laws and institutions of the U.S., and international rights as an internally oppressed people—up to and including the right of secession.

Katrina's Legacy: White Racism and Black Reconstruction in New Orleans and the Gulf Coast is offered as a weapon, a tactic in the ideological battle with right-wing think tanks, right-wing organizers, and right-wing cadre who are leading the counterrevolution. These tightly organized and highly motivated forces of reaction can only be challenged by the most thoughtful, strategic, revolutionary war of position from the Left, to shift the terms of the debate, and to create a framework for a new popular resistance to challenge the Right, to challenge the U.S. empire.

Eric Mann

Los Angeles, CA

Section I

History Can Guide Us

Then came this battle called the Civil War, beginning in Kansas in 1854, and ending with the presidential elections of 1876—twenty awful years. The slave went free; stood a brief moment in the sun; then moved back again towards slavery. The whole weight of America was thrown to color caste. [3]

W.E.B. Du Bois, *Black Reconstruction in America*

But what shall we do with the Negroes after they are free? I can hardly believe that the South and North can live in peace unless we get rid of the Negroes. Certainly they cannot, if we don't get rid of the Negroes who we have armed and disciplined and who have fought with us, to the amount, I believe, of some 150,000 men. I believe that it would be better to export them all to some fertile country with a good climate, which they could have to themselves. You have been a staunch friend of the [Black] race from the time you first advised me to enlist them in New Orleans...What then are our difficulties in sending the Blacks away?[4]

President Abraham Lincoln to General Benjamin F. Butler (April 1865)

We need new friends, we need new allies. We need to expand the civil rights struggle to a higher level—to the level of human rights. Whenever you are in a civil rights struggle, whether you know it or not, you are confining yourself to the jurisdiction of Uncle Sam. No one from the outside world can speak out in your behalf as long as your struggle is a civil rights struggle. Civil rights comes within the domestic affairs of this country. All of our African brothers and our Asian brothers and our Latin-American brothers cannot open their mouths and interfere in the domestic affairs of the United States.

But the United Nations has a Universal Declaration of Human Rights; it has a committee that deals in human rights. When you expand the civil rights struggle to the level of human rights, you can then take the case of the Black man in this country before the nations in the United Nations. You can take it before the General Assembly. You can take Uncle Sam before a world court. But the only level you can do it on is the level of human rights...

Uncle Sam's hands are dripping with blood, dripping with the blood of the Black man in this country. He's the earth's number-one hypocrite. He has the audacity—yes, he has—imagine him posing as the leader of the free world. The free world! Expand the civil rights struggle to the level of human rights. Take it into the United Nations, where our African brothers can throw their weight on our side, where our Asian brothers can throw their weight on our side, where our Latin-American brothers can throw their weight on our side, and where 800 million Chinamen are sitting there waiting to throw their weight on our side.[5]

Malcolm X, "The Ballot or the Bullet," (April 3, 1963, Baltimore, Maryland)

The System Fails, the Movement Regroups

In Louisiana, just a few weeks after Category Five Hurricane Katrina struck New Orleans and the Gulf Coast, 49 movement organizations from throughout the region met to develop a common strategy and tactical plan. Gathering in Baton Rouge, they formed the People's Hurricane Relief Fund and Oversight Coalition (PHRF). Their main goal: to create a Black-led, multiracial, progressive reconstruction plan for New Orleans and the region that could challenge the white, corporate take-over already underway. The group also discussed how to use the painful example of the human-made disaster, the racism of the Bush Administration, and the vacillation and spinelessness of the Democrats to help create a new movement with an independent, community-based program. This meeting led to a follow-up meeting in St. Helena Island, South Carolina in November, many nationwide support rallies, marches, demonstrations, press conferences, progressive legislation introduced by the Congressional Black Caucus, neighborhood efforts headed up by groups such as Common Ground and Mama D. This work continued into a December 8-10, 2005 meeting, "Survivors Assembly and March for the Right of Return." There have been actions to stop evictions, to stop police brutality and to punish police who abandoned prisoners during the hurricane, efforts to get the Federal Emergency Management Agency (FEMA) to pay for housing and hotels for the survivors, fights for freedom of information, and fights for union jobs with prevailing wages. It has continued through the mayoral election of April/May 2006 and accelerated with demands for a major expansion and strengthening of the levee system as the hurricane season approaches as well as the first anniversary of Katrina.

When the first version of *Katrina's Legacy* was written in September of 2005, one of the great fears of grassroots groups in New Orleans was that the suffering of the people, especially because they were Black people, would be soon forgotten, long before remedies could be proposed and a coherent movement could be constructed. But in fact, the New Orleans story has had surprising staying power on the front pages of the newspapers, and the grassroots groups, often carrying out similar but different tactical plans, have managed to keep the demands for the Right of Return and for a viable, Black-led rebuilding of New Orleans in the face of the power structure. Whether those demands can be translated into actual policies is the challenge facing all of us who organize to build social movements during these dark and dangerous times; but the groups in New Orleans are to be commended for keeping up the public pressure as they fight for a broader united front to turn demands into changes in people's lives.

As the PHRF and other grassroots groups propose an alternative, Black-led development plan for the Gulf Coast, they face an even greater danger: the plan of the Bush Administration and the two-party elite to "bulldoze New Orleans," drive out the majority Black population, give the city "a smaller footprint," and rebuild the city as a depopulated, sanitized, suburban theme park with a majority white, affluent population.

The so-called "natural" disaster of Hurricane Katrina is actually the human-made disaster of U.S. imperialism in general and the Bush oligarchy in particular—where global warming (driven by the emissions of the U.S. economy), imperialist overextension in Iraq, the cruelest versions of structural and individual racism, the crisis of the cities, and the national oppression of Black people (in particular in the South) all tragically intersect.

There are historical moments when a convergence of events creates a governing crisis for the system and the ruling class loses public support and legitimacy. As a result, we are presented with an opportunity. Movement forces that previously have been weak and divided can find a rallying cry and a moment of focus to launch a programmatic and ideological struggle that pushes the system back on its heels. New Orleans—the city, but also as a symbol for the greater Gulf Coast, the Black movement in the South, the Black movement in the U.S., and the Third World within and without the territorial boundaries of the U.S.—offers such a historical challenge and opportunity.

Strategic Framework

Given the enormous number of righteous demands generated by grassroots groups—including demands to bring back intact the dispersed Black population of New Orleans, and for housing and renters' rights, income support, restrictions on police brutality, a survivors fund, massive environmental clean up and reconstruction, and community oversight of all redevelopment efforts—a key question is, what are some broader strategic demands that can frame a comprehensive program of Black liberation and community revitalization?

Imperialism as a system operates by oppressing and super-exploiting whole nations and peoples, and it uses the ideology of racism to subjugate peoples of color throughout the world. Therefore, an international, anti-imperialist united front is not simply a slogan but a strategy in which to situate the many creative demands generated at the grassroots. The goal: to unite all who can be united to isolate the Bush Administration and the Right Wing of the Democratic Party. Four strategic demands can give focus and clarity to the many other specific demands generated by the grassroots.

1) *The right of self-determination and the highest level of material aid, under community control, to the oppressed Black people in the Gulf Coast.* The Right of Return is the key to any form of self-determination, for without a returning Black majority there can be no Black power, and Black dispersal will only perpetuate white supremacy.

2) *An environmental justice/public health framework* to rebuild the city in a way to dramatically reduce greenhouse gases and air toxins, and to reverse ecological disintegration and global warming. Before Katrina, New Orleans and the Gulf Coast were known for "Cancer Alley" and a toxic soup of industrial emissions, while the ravages of global warming were trivialized as natural disasters common to the region's history and folklore. As Halliburton and the corporate raiders seize upon New Orleans as a corporate welfare project, there must be an alternative vision of a green city to offer an aggressive challenge to the ecological catastrophe

inherent in present capitalist methods of industrial production, transportation, urban construction, and an obsessive consumer culture that seduces the oppressed to participate in the planet's destruction.

3) *A frontal challenge to the national security state and the racist prison system.* FEMA is not just incompetent, but it operates under the authority of the Office of Homeland Security. The New Orleans police were not just derelict in their duties; they used armed force to suppress Black people seeking food and shelter even during the hurricane. New Orleans' Black poor are imprisoned at rates only comprehensible as human rights abuses, and yet even in the midst of Katrina and its aftermath, the shooting and locking up of poor Black people took precedence over rescuing them. The focus on jobs, housing, and income cannot be separated from the harsh reality that Black people in the U.S. are an incarcerated people. Freeing the Black prisoners must be pushed to the center of the debate about a third Black-led Reconstruction.

4) *The immediate withdrawal of all U.S. troops from Iraq.* As we speak, more than 2,500 U.S. soldiers, and more than 30,000 (with some estimates as high as 100,000) Iraqis, most of them civilians, have died in the U.S. invasion and occupation of Iraq, and tens of thousands more have been severely injured for life. As this is written, a group of U.S. marines is facing trial for the execution-style assassinations of 24 unarmed Iraqi civilians in Haditha—an ethical and political catastrophe for the

war of occupation to rival the atrocities of Abu Ghraib prison. Still, the bloodbath continues unabated as the U.S. occupation has now generated a bitter civil war. The U.S. government initially allocated billions for construction companies in New Orleans and now, to fund its immoral war of aggression in Iraq, is dramatically cutting social programs to pay for its capitalist objectives at home and abroad. The U.S. policies of invasion of Iraq and support for Israel's occupation and persecution of the Palestinian people has now led to the humanitarian disaster of Israel's carpet bombing and invasion of Lebanon. The tradition of the Student Non-Violent Coordinating Committee (SNCC)'s "Hell No, We Won't Go" refusal to fight in the war in Vietnam, and the strong internationalist politics of Malcolm X and Martin Luther King Jr. can guide today's movement and provide a coherent internationalist and human rights frame for demand development.

These four strategic demands can provide a framework for programmatic coherence in the current political context. A discussion of counterhegemonic programmatic demands is elaborated in Section II of *Katrina's Legacy*.

The Historical Achievements of the Black Liberation Movement—Lessons for a New Reconstruction

We are living in an historical period in which the greatest blow against the progressive movement and the Left is the theft of the history of our intellectual, moral, and political victories against the system—in particular, the efforts to obliterate the profound contributions of the Black Liberation Movement. The possibility for any multiracial, international movement of resistance to the profound racism in the Gulf Coast situation lies in rebuilding this historical record.

The foundation for resistance has already been built by the abolitionist work of Nat Turner, Harriet Tubman, Frederick Douglass, Sojourner Truth, and John Brown; the heroic Black Reconstruction Movement of 1865-1877; the century of struggle against Jim Crow; the 1950s-1970s Civil Rights and Black Liberation Movement, encompassing the work of SNCC, CORE, SCLC, Deacons for Defense, the Black Panthers, and the Gary Indiana Black Political Convention of 1972. Throughout the 20th century, this resistance has been framed by the intellectual and strategic work of Marcus Garvey, W.E.B. Du Bois, Paul Robeson, Harry Haywood, Fannie Lou Hamer, Ella Baker, Malcolm X, Martin Luther King, and Amiri Baraka. It has been supported by the Black community's many dedicated allies, including Yuri Kochiyama, Reies López Tijerina, Cesar Chavez, Mickey Schwerner, and Andy Goodman. Always an issue on the international stage, it has received powerful Third World support from the Pan African congresses, the Bandung Conference of non-aligned nations, the Chinese and Cuban revolutions, and the victory of the Vietnamese National Liberation Front.

But today, the Black commuity is under attack, isolated, and lacking a coherent ideology of resistance or Black United Front forms of organization. In this context, re-establishing the historical record is a central tactic in reversing the despair and beginning to go on the offensive.

The First Reconstruction: Program for Emancipation (1865-1877)

In 1865, less than 150 years ago, when Black people in the South won legal freedom from slavery, millions of Black women and men were thrust onto the historical stage. A Black political class emerged, able to create an alliance of Black freed men and women, some southern poor whites and workers, northern abolitionists, and Radical Republicans. This united front coalition drafted a program to consolidate the victory over the rebellious and racist South, and passed some of the most progressive legislation and social policies in U.S. history.

This plan was based on the material power of more than 150,000 armed Blacks who had rebelled against slavery and fought with the North in the Civil War, backed by four million more potentially-armed Blacks.

Imagine a period in which more than four million Black women and men, after three centuries of slavery, are instantly "freed." They enter the post Civil War world with little history of training in politics, no history of even the relative freedom-within-oppression of a colonized people in Africa, no permitted relationships with whites except an always terrorized set of adaptations and charades as tactics of self-defense. A progressive, revolutionary Black political class and multi-class mass movement emerged, based on the small but influential strata of free Blacks who had owned property and learned the skills of bourgeois society combined with the massive power of the former slaves. Imagine what a revolution it was to have former slaves, women and men, leading a political movement after centuries of being denied their families, their right to read or speak their mind, the right to travel outside of the plantation. Their limited history of common activity was restricted by the yoke of bondage to field slave slow-downs and sabotage, the miracle of the underground railroad, and the galvanizing, brave, brief, slave rebellions that were passed on as folklore by word of mouth as the ultimate model of hope. This consciousness, leadership, and organization was geometrically expanded in a period of a few short years, 1860-1865, in which Black slaves rose up against their overextended masters, fled the plantations, enlisted in the Union army, and were given freedom, training, and most importantly, guns.

What made Reconstruction so revolutionary was that it called for a true bourgeois democratic revolution—to grant the slaves full equality, to grant workers of all races the right to organize and make demands on government and their employers, and to militarily restrict and suppress the former planter class in the South, which was intent upon a counterrevolution. Among these forces who could form a united front for Reconstruction were the masses of the Black multi-class nation in the South just freed from bondage, free Blacks in the North, southern white workers, northern white workers, and the northern white middle and upper class progressives represented by the Radical Republicans.

But from the beginning, the Reconstruction movement faced powerful enemies. First, its temporary ally, the growing monopoly capitalist/imperialist class in the North entering its robber baron phase, had little interest in freeing the slaves or granting a multi-racial working class democracy. Rather, it saw its main enemy as the feudal/capitalist class in the South, and was willing to make temporary alliances to consolidate its victory in the war. From the outset, there were conservative forces in the North who anticipated re-uniting with the plantocracy, who shared a white supremacist hatred of the Blacks, and who simply wanted to make sure that the new alliance was under Northern control. Thus, in order to succeed, the Reconstruction movement had to somehow maintain the support of Northern monopoly capitalism for democratic rights for Blacks, as it also struggled for full democracy against the interests of the corporate class north and south—a very difficult tactical plan.

In the midst of this white collusion came the Radical Republicans, men and women, Black and white, of great principle, who saw the plight of women, the working class, and "the Negroes" as causes in themselves, not as tactical decisions to advance their class interests, but as part of a broader philosophy of capitalist reform. They were worried about the unchecked power of the growing monopoly capital, and saw the vaunted ideals of the United States as a cover for white racist aggrandizement. Many of them had been elected to the United States Senate and House of Representatives. Imagine them almost as a true Third Party, a left caucus within the Republicans fighting the conservative wing of the Republicans, and the reactionary party, the Democrats. Due to their great initiative, for about a decade they were able to drive a broad united front led by the Republican party. Their objective was to convince the powerful northern capitalists that in order to effectively suppress the southern reactionaries and to restore the "Union" based on a victory in the Civil War, they needed to allow Black suffrage and full democratic rights for Black people—the effective right to vote, to free assembly, to run for office, to organize politically, and to pass progressive social and economic legislation. The historic Black Reconstruction Movement had a clear program that included the full enfranchisement of Black people in the South, the election of Black and progressive people to office, a major land reform program to bring land back to those who had tilled it as slaves, and profound infusions of funds for Black public education and training. This overall progressive program reached out to, and for a moment included, significant numbers of poor whites who for centuries had been the volunteer militia of "slave catchers" for the slave owners but now, without land or jobs and faced with the material reality of Black power, sought the possibility of a multiracial working class movement led by former Black slaves.[6]

This miraculous decade, directly following and as a result of the Union victory over the Confederacy in the U.S. Civil War, was defined by new legal status for Black people. The 13th, 14th, and 15th amendments to the U.S. Constitution outlawed slavery, conferred U.S. citizenship upon Black people, and extended the franchise to Black males.

In 1865, Congress established the Bureau of Refugees, Freedmen, and Abandoned Lands, known as the Freedmen's Bureau, to assist emancipated slaves. According to Du Bois, the program of the Freedmen's Bureau entailed specific responsibilities: "the relief of physical suffering, the overseeing of the beginnings of free labor, the buying and selling of land, the establishment of schools, the paying of bounties, the administration of justice, and the financiering of all these activities."[7]

In 1866, at the initiation of a Black delegation led by Frederick Douglass, Congress passed a Civil Rights Act, conferring citizenship upon Black Americans and guaranteeing equal rights with whites—overriding a veto by Lincoln's successor President Andrew Johnson. In 1867, again overriding President Johnson, Congress passed the First Reconstruction Act of 1867 that established military districts to oversee the progress of Reconstruction, to militarily protect the former slaves from bloody retaliation, and to suppress the newly formed Ku Klux Klan and other counter-revolutionary white supremacist organizations. The Second Reconstruction Act required the registration of eligible voters. The Third and Fourth Acts clarified that existing civil governments no longer had legal standing in the South and reinforced the authority of the federal military to enforce the civil rights laws that demanded enfranchisement of former slaves. Komozi Woodard describes some of the on-the-ground achievements of Reconstruction.

> In some counties in the South, blacks enjoyed considerable social and economic benefits from Black political power. For instance, in Beaufort, South Carolina, black rice workers struck for higher wages and decent living conditions. In light of black political power in the state, Governor Chamberlain refused the rich planters' demand

> that he send in troops to crush black labor resistance. Moreover, the black workers were emboldened by the support of such black elected officials as Congressman Robert Smalls, the civil war hero.[8]

The fight against counter-revolution was a critical component of the Reconstruction period from the beginning. The tragedy of the assassination of President Abraham Lincoln in 1865 (who had his own vacillation on the issues of full democratic rights for the freed Black slaves) was his replacement by Andrew Johnson, the Vice President at the time, the reactionary ally of the South, and the mortal enemy of Black people. Johnson was adamantly opposed by the Radical Republicans in the Congress, at a time when the capitalist class had not fully consolidated its power in the "chief executive's" office. The Radical Republicans led a process of impeachment, bringing Johnson up on charges of subverting the constitution with the goal of removing him from office. They came close to succeeding except for the pro-slavery votes of some members of their own party. Senators Thaddeus Stevens, who came to the impeachment proceedings against Johnson in his last dying days, and Charles Sumner, led the almost-successful effort to remove Johnson from office. Sumner railed against Johnson's treachery:

> This is one of the last great battles with slavery. Driven from the legislative chambers, driven from the field of war, this monstrous power has found a refuge in the executive mansion, where, in utter disregard of the Constitutution and laws, it seeks to exercise its ancient far-reaching sway... Andrew Johnson is the impersonation of the tyrannical slave power. In him it lives again. He is the lineal successor

> of John C. Calhoun and Jefferson Davis, and he gathers about him the same supporters. [9]

While the Reconstruction movement was able to achieve great gains, the treachery of the Johnson presidency and its alliance with armed southern whites prevented the achievement of a key demand of Reconstruction leaders—Reparations, in the form of redistribution of land from the plantation system to a new system of Black land ownership. The 800,000 acres of abandoned Confederate land that were to be distributed by the Bureau of Refugees, Freedmen, and Abandoned Lands never reached the masses of former slaves but, instead, ended up in the hands of Confederate soldiers who were granted amnesty by Johnson. The speculative developers who stole and profited from lang originally intnded for Blacks are the ancestors of the Halliburtons, Bechtels adn Flours that are explointing the Bulf Coast today.

Land redistribution was fundamental to the initial Reconstruction program. The progressive Black leadership of the early Reconstruction period was exemplified by the twenty Black ministers who met in January 1865 in Savannah, Georgia with General Sherman and the Secretary of War to negotiate terms of resettlement for freed slaves. Asked how the freedmen might best maintain their freedom, spokesperson Garrison Frazier answered: "The way we can best take care of ourselves is to have land, and turn it and till it by our labor."[10]

Within two weeks Sherman instituted Special Field Order No. 15. It stated "the islands of Charleston south, the abandoned rice fields along the rivers for thirty miles back from the sea...are set apart for the settlement of Negroes..."[11] By the summer, the Freedmen's Bureau had distributed

400,000 acres of abandoned Confederate land to 40,000 freedmen (as Sherman's Order stated "each family shall have a plot of not more than forty acres"). But President Johnson was determined to undermine the new Reconstruction alliance and prevent any form of Reparations at any cost. By the beginning of the following year, Johnson had rescinded all distributed land titles and ordered the return of lands to pardoned Confederate soldiers.

The achievements of the Radical Republicans and the self-activity of free Blacks and freed slaves are reflected in a tumultuous 12 years during which democratic rights were granted and public education was established as an objective for all freed slaves through out the South. The southern white hatred of both "the North" and "the federal government" that exists to this day stems from this revolutionary period in which the white supremacists and plantocracy were, for once, under restriction and even temporary subjugation. The Black-led Reconstruction movement offers a model of hope and shapes the terms of Black resistance and multiracial left organizing to this day. It is the subject of one of the greatest books in the history of the written word, *Black Reconstruction in America* by W.E.B. Du Bois. Du Bois' work serves as the fundamental theoretical and analytical frame of *Katrina's Legacy*.

The First Racist Counterrevolution: Jim Crow Apartheid (1877-1955)

This is the story of how a reactionary Democrat/conservative Republican alliance of the northern imperialists and the southern plantocracy worked to overthrow Reconstruction and send the Black masses back to virtual slavery at the hands of southern white barbarism.

As an oppressed people, a "nation within a nation" as Du Bois described Black people in the South, a large but militarily outnumbered minority, the Black movement desperately needed the protracted, permanent protection of federal troops to allow them to consolidate political and economic opportunity and power and to achieve full democratic rights. Tragically, the unique and fragile experiment of Black Reconstruction begun in 1865 was overturned through a process of gradual erosion, culminating twelve years later in a counter-revolutionary victory of southern planters and conservative Northern capitalists, the so-called "Hayes-Tilden compromise of 1877." In the national presidential election of 1876, the vote was so close between the conservative Republican, Rutherford B. Hayes, and the reactionary Democrat, Samuel Tilden, that the virtual tie was thrown into the House of Representatives for resolution. In return for the Democrats agreeing that Hayes would assume the presidency, they won a far greater victory, the agreement that the new Republican administration would withdraw federal troops from the South and allow the counter-revolution of northern and southern capital to proceed with full force. That ugly backroom deal allowed southern white landowners and other members of its ruling class to re-impose a plantation economy based on the superexploitation of Black wage labor, and to unleash a bloodbath against the Black masses to forcibly impose white power and a literal police-state fascism.

Benjamin Wade, a Radical Republican congressman, explained his outrage at the betrayal of Black people by the Republican majority and Rutherford B. Hayes and predicted the unmitigated horrors to be inflicted on the former slaves.

> You know with what untiring zeal I labored for the emancipation of the slaves of the South and to procure justice for them before and during the time I was in Congress, and I supposed Governor Hayes was in full accord with me on this subject. But I have been deceived, betrayed, and even humiliated in the course he has taken to a degree I do not have language to express. I feel that to have emancipated these people and then leave them unprotected would be a crime as infamous as to have reduced them to slavery when they were free.[12]

The economic system of neo-slavery was reinforced by a series of laws that began with the Black Codes, which criminalized every aspect of Black everyday life, and evolved into the Jim Crow system of formal apartheid, creating a reign of terror against Black people for a full century. This brutal system was fully supported by northern "progressives" from Republican Teddy Roosevelt to Democrat Franklin Delano Roosevelt. The segregation laws extended the ability of the United White Settler States to construct U.S. capitalism and imperialism through the superexpolitation of Blacks as an oppressed people, an oppressed nationality within the U.S.

Why did the North become so reactionary? Why did the post-war "Union" evolve as an imperialist, white settler state instead of a multiracial capitalist democracy? Why did the white North reward its enemies, the white secessionists whom it restored to power, and punish its friends, the Black slaves without whom the North could never have defeated the South in the first place?

Amiri Baraka in his essay on Du Bois, explicates the thesis that it was the representatives of northern imperialist capital who were the prime movers in the re-enslavement of the Blacks, while the white southerners were its main mechanism of implementation.

> The slaves were not peasants; they were slave workers, except for the small groups of free Blacks and the overwhelming number of white farmers in the South. When chattel slavery was destroyed the Black struggle became a land struggle...so that the slaves could become a class of small entrepreneurs. But with the betrayal of Reconstruction by the newly imperialist forces of northern corporate industrial power, the land (the vaunted 40 acres and a mule) was seized by Wall Street (by 1873, 80% of southern lands were owned by northern capital) whose southern outpost was Atlanta.
>
> The Mexican War of 1848, the ongoing pacification of the Native peoples, was followed by big capital allying itself temporarily with northern abolitionist democracy, as Du Bois called it, and the multi-national working class both Black and White. Once the 200,000 Black troops had completely destroyed the Plantation Owners as a class, the superficial move towards full democracy and land settlement, education, equal citizenship rights was tolerated until big capital secured full control of southern land and remaining institutions and the White middle class, the small businessmen, politicians, overseers, small farmers, were transformed into a comprador for rising Wall Street based U.S. imperialism.[13]

The term "comprador" used by Baraka is a Marxist formulation explained most effectively by Mao-Tse-tung in his *Analysis of the Classes in Chinese Society.*[14] A comprador bourgeoisie is not an independent capitalist class, but rather, the functionaries for the imperialist class within a subjugated nation. They get their class power from their masters. The compradors have been classically reflected in the native colonial puppet governments or colonized bureaucracies that served their British, French, Japanese, and U.S. rulers in the Third World. In the case of the United States after the Civil War, the entire white caste (in a dual caste system of Black and white) was deputized to re-enslave Black people and do the bidding of Northern capitalists who they hated, but far less than they hated the Blacks. (The history of how large sections of the white working class in the South and North became allies of white capital and enemies of Black workers is a story unto itself.)

In one of history's biting ironies, it was the white South that eventually transformed and took over imperialism itself, turning the former Northern victors of the Civil War into their new subordinated co-conspirators—reflected in the long-standing power of the Dixiecrats, the Democratic Leadership Council's good old boys Bill Clinton and Al Gore, and the new Sun Belt Republican cowboys of the Barry Goldwater, Ronald Reagan, George Bush, Sr. and George W. Bush, Jr. variety. Rather than the capitalist North eventually bringing racial equality and democracy to the South (which it's majority never really wanted or supported in the first place),. it was the South that imposed a xenophobic chauvinist racist reality on the entire United States. As Du Bois observed, the entire U.S. was "turned into a prototype of the south."

The Second Reconstruction: The Civil Rights Revolution (1955-1975)

One hundred years after the end of the Civil War and almost a century after the white South staged its first counterrevolution, Congress passed the 1964 Civil Rights Act and the 1965 Voting Rights Act. These critical reforms were conscious choices by U.S. ruling circles at the national level to repair the profound damage to "the system" of the Hayes-Tilden compromise and the ravages of Jim Crow. They were the product of decades of post-World War II militant civil rights resistance and a growing world communist and anti-imperialist Left, winning converts in the Third World over the overt racism of the U.S. As with the First Reconstruction, a minority of Liberal Democrats during the Second Reconstruction were truly committed to the broader cause of full democratic rights for Blacks, and an antiracist, antiwar capitalist democracy. As the Radical Republicans before them, they were eventually suppressed by their party and voted out of office by an increasingly racist and conservative electorate.

In 1965-1968, during a revolution of rising expectations, Black people participated in urban rebellions in Watts, Detroit, Harlem, Newark, Cleveland, and Washington D.C. For many young people today, it may be hard to imagine that Black-led rebellions took place in more than 458 cities between 1967 and 1969 alone.[15] During that period, there was considerable international support for the demands of Black people; the Soviet Union, People's Republic of China, and Third World nations throughout Asia, Africa, and Latin America, as well as many progressive students in European universities, voiced their solidarity. There even was significant, though minority, white sympathy for why Black people would rebel.[16] This perspective argued that centuries of racist abuse had provoked Black outrage. It viewed police brutality, poverty, and structural racism, including the assassinations of Malcolm X and Martin Luther King, as the causes of Black rebellion.[17]

In retrospect, the profound mass militancy and structural victories of the Civil Rights Movement and the Black Liberation Movement can be understood as a Second Black Reconstruction. During this Second Reconstruction, a broad united front of Black organizations, representing different social classes and perspectives, and despite personal and political conflicts, was able to unite around a clear and popularly understood and supported program. From 1955 to 1975, "the two decades of the sixties," there was a strong and exploding Black movement; a growing Latino/Chicano upsurge, reflected in La Raza Unida Party, the Brown Berets, the Young Lords, Reies López Tijerina's fight for land in the Southwest, and the Chicano Moratorium Against the War in Vietnam; Asian/Pacific Islander movements, from the Red Guards to broad Chinatown coalitions supporting U.S. normalization with the People's Republic of China; the resurgence of the Indigenous movements with the great contribution of the American Indian Movement; and large antiracist organizations of white students such as Students for a Democratic Society. Virtually all of the leaders of those movements acknowledged their debt of gratitude and formative thinking to the leadership of the Black movement. This multiracial, Black-led Left was a major force in U.S. society. It was both in unity and in struggle with a significant liberal wing of the Democratic Party, many of whose members were elected during the 1960s and 1970s in opposition to the Dixiecrats, to the "moderates" who conciliated with them, and to the war in Vietnam that had been escalated by Democratic presidents John Kennedy and Lyndon Johnson.

The Black Liberation/Reconstruction program included: an end to police brutality and proposals for civilian and (Black) community control of the police; comprehensive jobs and social services, including the concept raised by the Communist Party USA during the 1930s of "jobs or income now," federal "anti-poverty" programs that included dramatic expansion of benefits and eligibility for Aid to Families With Dependent Children, Head Start programs for pre-school children and massive funding for Black and inner city schools; a breakthrough in large-scale hiring of Black people for private and public sector jobs; and powerful government protections for voting rights and against discrimination.

These demands were framed by the two strategic demands the system hated the most:

- "Black Power," reflected in the demand for Black control of community institutions, a Black homeland and Black self-determination.

- "U.S. Out of Vietnam," the growing sentiment in Black communities to bring Black (and Latino, Asian/Pacific Islander, Indigenous, and working class white) soldiers home and allow the Vietnamese people to exercise the right of self-determination.

Many "non-violent" militant civil rights activists, especially before the 1963 March on Washington, initially felt that the implementation of the equal protection clause of the 14th Amendment (full equality, civil rights under the system, and full democratic rights) would eventually be accepted by the system and solve the structural problems of white racism and Black subordination. But with the Kennedy Administration's weak protections for civil rights workers and its conciliation with southern Dixiecrats and the treacherous role played by J. Edgar Hoover and the FBI to sabotage rather than enforce civil rights laws, these young activists came to understand just how revolutionary the simple demand for "equality" and an end to racial segregation proved to be.

Many militant reformers were transformed into revolutionaries by the lynchings of the Klan, the blows of police billy clubs (in the North and in the South), the assaults of high-powered water hoses, and the racist killings that just would not stop—from Emmett Till to Medgar Evers to the four young girls who were the victims of the Birmingham Church bombing to Goodman, Schwerner, and Chaney to the murders of Malcolm X, Martin Luther King, and Fred Hampton, and yes, the assassinations of John and Bobby Kennedy.

In 1972, poet and revolutionary organizer Amiri Baraka and Gary, Indiana Mayor Richard Hatcher helped convene one of the broadest Black united fronts in U.S. history: the National Black Political Convention in Gary, Indiana. This convention, organized under the concept of a Black Agenda, generated a series of comprehensive political demands, including holding Black elected officials accountable to the Black community.

> Some eight thousand African Americans (three thousand of whom were official delegates) arrived...[at] the "Gary Convention." A sea of Black faces chanted, "It's Nation Time! It's Nation Time!" No one in the room had ever seen anything like this before. The radical Black nationalists clearly won the day; moderates who supported integration and backed the Democratic Party were in the minority.[18]

Also during the late 1960s and early 1970s, the Black Panther Party's Ten Point Program generated a comprehensive and radical view, punctuated by a quote from the Declaration of Independence in which the U.S. "seceded" from England. This was followed by the tenth "key" demand:

> We want land, bread, housing, education, clothing, justice, and peace. As our major political objective, a United Nations supervised plebiscite to be held throughout the Black colony in which only Black colonial subjects will be allowed to participate, for the purpose of determining the will of Black people as to their destiny.[19]

The Black movement during the mid-1960s and 1970s developed a strong internationalist and Third World orientation. It called for solidarity with the people of Africa, support for the anti-Apartheid movement, and the most militant opposition to the Vietnam War. Muhammad Ali's agitational masterpiece, "No Viet Cong Ever Called Me a N——," mobilized Black and

Latino youth, many of whom were already enlisted, to turn on their own officers and refuse to kill Vietnamese youth fighting for self-determination. The connection between racism and oppression at home and abroad was highlighted by SNCC's cry, "Hell No, We Won't Go" to the war in Vietnam, Martin Luther King's "the United States is the worst purveyor of violence in the world," and the 1970 Chicano Moratorium in Los Angeles, the largest Latino antiwar demonstration with more than 30,000 participants who chanted, "Raza Sí, Guerra No!"

This movement had a worldview and an international strategy. It had significant and powerful grassroots power on the ground, functional unity between Black groups themselves (with, of course, tremendous tension and conflict), and a multiracial multinational alliance that included significant antiracist white support and involvement.

The Second Racist Counterrevolution: The New Right (1980-Present)

The story of the Second Racist Counterrevolution that followed the Second Black Reconstruction begins with three simple points: (1) it happened; (2) we are still living through it; and (3) New Orleans in the era of Katrina is a powerful and painful reflection of its impact.

Today the Black community in the U.S. has been under attack from a ferocious counterrevolution that began almost before the civil rights revolution got off the ground. The "white backlash," which included white voters abandoning the Democratic Party in droves, began from the first day the federal government sent any troops to protect civil rights workers, the first day one Black person received a job through an affirmative action program, and the first day one Black person was registered to vote through civil rights organizing.

By 1964, the country was split between a passionate movement for civil rights and an hysterical and frenzied white backlash. The Democratic Party, through the election of Lyndon Johnson, tried desperately to hold together a white and Black coalition. But, despite an unusual outpouring of decency among a significant minority of whites (including some in the South), the vast majority of white people and white voters were and still remain rabidly anti-Black.

Historically, southern whites in particular had voted for the Democrats for a century to punish the Republicans (the party of Lincoln) for defeating the Confederacy in the Civil War and for sending federal troops to the South after the war to enforce the 13th, 14th, and 15th amendments. Many southern whites saw Lyndon Johnson, a southerner from Texas, as a traitor for his leadership in passing civil rights legislation; still they voted Democrat in 1964 in a last ditch attempt to support the racist Dixiecrats who controlled every southern state and virtually all the key positions in Congress. But, after the passage of the 1964 Civil Rights Act and the 1965 Voting Rights Act (and after just three years of the federal government's attempts to enforce those laws) the white South bolted en masse to the now thoroughly racist Republican Party, where it has wallowed ever since.

By the 1968 presidential election, Republican Richard Nixon campaigned on a "Southern Strategy" that assured the white South, through the racially coded discourse of "law and order," that he would not enforce civil rights laws, but would use police violence to suppress Black urban protests and rebellions. The white South rewarded him by voting Republican for the first time in its history. But the Nixon vote was not even the worst development. In that same election, George Wallace, Governor of Alabama and a champion of apartheid, bolted from the Democratic Party, ran on a states' rights and "defense of segregation" platform, and argued to white voters that even the Republicans were not racist enough. Although Nixon carried most of the southern states, Wallace won the electoral votes in the Gulf Coast states—Alabama, Mississippi, Louisiana, Arkansas, and Georgia. Nixon barely won the election, receiving only 43 percent of the popular vote. Hubert Humphrey, the Democrat, received 42 percent, and Wallace received 13 percent of the vote, which included many white working class votes from the North, where white anger about Black power and the urban rebellions had reached a fever pitch.

Just as the First Counterrevolution resulted in the establishment of Jim Crow laws, the Second Counterrevolution did not simply aim to slowdown the Civil Rights Movement. Instead, it inflicted a subsequent reign of terror against Black people to reverse, not simply halt, the expansion of civil and economic rights. Richard Nixon and George Wallace's plans worked. The Republicans, quickly followed by the Democrats, totally abandoned the demands of the Black community. With the assassinations of Malcolm X and Martin Luther King, the Black movement was denied the "Black messiah" that J. Edgar Hoover and the white establishment feared (and played a role in extinguishing).

A few years later, in 1978, the racist movement used the Bakke legal case to launch a brilliantly manipulative attack on affirmative action. Alan Bakke, a white medical school applicant to the U.C. Davis School of Medicine, claimed he was a victim of the now infamous concept of "reverse discrimination." The Supreme Court upheld his claim by a 5 to 4 vote, paving the way for the anti-affirmative action movement. By 1980 came the rise of Ronald Reagan and Margaret Thatcher, and an international right-wing counterrevolution based on neoliberalism and counterinsurgency was in full swing.

By the late 1970s and early 1980s, the Civil Rights Movement was in full retreat. Many of its strongest leaders had been killed or imprisoned through the work of COINTELPRO, a government counterinsurgency program that infiltrated leftist groups, caused internal splits and wars in the movement, and assassinated Black revolutionaries (not unlike the current surveillance programs that use September 11 as their pretext). Both the Republican and Democratic parties—opportunistically seeking angry, conservative, and racist white voters—further abandoned Black voters (with the Democrats coming to realize they could still win Black votes without taking any risks to alienate white voters). In the meantime, the civil rights victories opened the door, both ideologically and materially, for a growing and influential Black capitalist class that began to repudiate the very politics that led to its ascension, many of whom became closely allied with "the white power structure" and the corporate agenda.

In the face of this rightward movement and massive government repression, many Black left organizations increased attacks on other Leftists with whom they did not agree, and a climate of sectarian infighting and vicious competition grew. Reduced to a shell of their former selves, with many former members dropping out and recanting their actual experiences, these groups were unable to generate new forms of mass resistance and unable to contemplate a new revolutionary path under the difficult conditions of the rise of the Right.

And yet, during the Reagan years, there were significant efforts at popular resistance that created new alliances. Black, Latino, Asian/Pacific Islander, and Indigenous organizations built "Third World" strategic alliances and began to advocate the formation of multiracial organizations.

A broad alliance between radical Black, Latino activists, labor groups, and Democratic Party reformers who wanted to fight the Right found a dynamic vehicle in Reverend Jesse Jackson's 1984 and 1988 presidential challenges. Jackson's candidacies, under the mantle of the "Rainbow Coalition," demonstrated the enormous potential for a Black-led, multiracial, progressive politics in the United States—and the possibility of aggressively challenging the Right.

In his 1988 campaign, Jackson and his Rainbow Coalition surprised the media and the political pundits. Initially written off as a marginal candidate, Jackson emerged in the Democratic Party primary season as a serious contender for the nomination. He attracted over 6.9 million votes—from urban Blacks and Latinos, poor rural whites, farmers and factory workers, feminists and gays, and from white progressives wanting to be part of an historic change. After early respectable losses in Iowa and New Hampshire, he won five southern states on Super Tuesday, March 8, 1988. On March 12, he won the caucus in his birth state of South Carolina and three days later finished second in his home state of Illinois. On March 26, Jackson stunned his closest challenger, Massachusetts Governor Michael Dukakis and the rest of the nation in the Michigan caucus: winning that northern industrial state with 55 percent of the vote, Jackson became the Democratic front-runner. Dukakis later recaptured the lead and the eventual nomination with strong showings in the second half of the primary season aided by an orchestrated white backlash and by the sabotage of Jackson by Democratic Party operatives.

Jackson went into the 1988 Democratic Convention hoping to be nominated for Vice President based on his very strong showing, coming in second to Dukakis and having defeated a host of white big name candidates from former Colorado Senator Gary Hart to astronaut and Ohio Senator John Glenn. Instead, the Democratic Party silenced him and his progressive demands. Jackson, compelled by calls of "party unity," and frightened by threats to isolate him from any positions of authority in the Party, chose to prioritize his future career aspirations and refused to challenge his suppression and marginalization. Shortly thereafter, Jackson disbanded the Rainbow Coalition he had built, and what had begun as an "independent" Rainbow Coalition challenging the rightward shift of the Democratic Party was sadly subsumed into the private property of an ambitious politician.

Following Ronald Reagan's 1984 rout of moderate liberal Walter Mondale, and in 1988, the pathetic performance of alleged liberal Michael Dukakis, and the racist and successful "Willie Horton" ploy of George Bush, Sr., the Democratic Party was losing white votes in droves, and was in a mood of outright panic.[20]

In 1985, an alliance of Democratic southern conservatives and Northern "neoliberals" formed the Democratic Leadership Council (DLC), to move the Democratic Party to the "center." Led by then-Governor of Arkansas Bill Clinton, Congressman Richard Gephardt (D-IN), and powerful tactician Al From, the New Democrats, as they advertised themselves, blamed the Democratic Party's internal crisis on "the liberals," advocated down playing discussions of civil rights, shed any "peace" identifications, advocated a "strong military" and suppressed and out-organized the declining liberal wing of the party. The goal was to woo back white voters from the Republicans with the "color blind" economics-oriented appeal: "It's the economy, stupid!"

But the Democrats' move to the right was not simply limited to "economic" and corporate issues. *Every year since 1968 the Democrats have moved further to the right on race.* This has transpired partially because Jesse Jackson and other progressive and Black Democrats have been unwilling to abandon, much less punish the Democrats by putting forth an independent program. They have refused to launch an independent *antiracist* campaign that could push the Party to defend civil rights, or, over time, bring former Democratic Black voters into the leadership of a third party. And while there exists the important Congressional Black Caucus and, on paper, a Democratic Progressive Caucus, neither of these forms has the ideological cohesiveness or political will to confront the conservatives the way the DLC openly and vociferously attacks the few remaining liberals in its own party.

By 1992, many Black elected officials and functionaries of the civil rights establishment, shaken by 12 years of Reagan and Bush with no end in sight, accepted Bill Clinton's assessment that, in order to win a national election, they needed *two* southern white men (Clinton and Gore) to work like hell to keep the remaining white voters inside the Democratic Party. In return for Black support (assurance of no civil rights pressure to his left), Clinton promised to provide a significant number of Black appointments and contracts if he won, which he did.

But rather than simply the racism of "benign neglect," (a proposal once made to Richard Nixon by then advisor and later Democratic Senator from New York, Daniel Moynihan) the Clinton Administration carried out vicious, right-wing policies that even the Republicans would not have considered by themselves. In 1996, the Clinton Administration undermined due process and *habeas corpus* by signing the "Anti-terrorism and Effective Death Penalty Act," which made it far harder for those convicted to overturn their death sentences, and opened the doors for Bush's later elaboration of the police state. Bill Clinton also campaigned on and carried out "ending welfare as we know it," which undermined federal social welfare protections that went back to FDR and the 1930s.

Clinton also personally sabotaged the movement in California to protect affirmative action programs at the University of California and other public institutions. From the outset of the right-wing assault on affirmative action as "reverse discrimination" and "promoting the unqualified" the Clinton Administration put many Democratic Party liberals on the defensive with the reactionary slogan, "Affirmative action, mend it don't end it" (as if Blacks had already gotten too much). Clinton undermined the work of California Democratic progressives by withholding promised Democratic Party funds from the "No on 209" (the anti-affirmative action initiative) Campaign in California.

Clinton actually worked to sabotage any effective defense of affirmative action, worried that it would hurt his own chances for re-election if the fight to defend affirmative action was given public visibility, as the initiative was on the same California ballot as the presidential one in 1996. In practice, Clinton gave ideological support to the racists. After this history of treachery, in his most disgraceful move, he bragged to Black supporters that he was "the first Black president."

The Clinton debacle was followed by the racist policies of Gore and then Kerry. Gore's refusal to challenge the 2000 presidential election results in Florida allowed the conservative Scalia/Thomas Supreme Court to throw the election to Bush. (Michael Moore's greatest historical contribution may be the inclusion in his documentary film *Fahrenheit 9/11* of footage showing Black Congress people protesting Bush's stolen presidency in the 2004 presidential election through voter fraud, only to have white, southern

Gore turn against his Black supporters. Gore chose instead to placate, once again, white southern and suburban voters who had voted against him, in the vain hope of securing their vote in some future election.)

In 2004, John Kerry ran a pathetic campaign altogether, and an even worse campaign with regard to the Black community and civil rights. Despite his color blind, racist appeal to white voters, Kerry and the Democratic Party were despised for their opportunism by this voting bloc, especially white males, who voted for George W. Bush in record numbers.* Tragically, even with Kerry's open contempt for Black voters and his wife Teresa Heinz's bizarre assertion that as a billionaire with family roots among the white colonialists from Zimbabwe she qualified as "an African American," Kerry was rewarded by receiving almost 90 percent of the national Black vote. Thus, the cynical tactic of the Democrats to take the Black vote for granted and chase after the white vote, with increasingly racist and reactionary appeals, does not presently cost them anything, and, in fact, perpetuates the political subjugation of Blacks. Similarly,

* The numbers are astounding. George Bush received 58 percent of white voters nationally, with Kerry receiving only 41 percent. Also nationally, Bush got 62 percent of the white male vote, and Kerry got only 37 percent. In the South, the numbers were off the charts (and increased the national average into which they are incorporated). Whites in the South voted 70 percent for Bush and 29 percent for Kerry, and white male voters in the South voted 72 percent for Bush and 27 percent for Kerry. These figures do not represent a two-party system among whites, but rather a white supremacy party, the Republicans, and a permanent minority party among more liberal and decent whites, the Democrats (who do nothing to earn the trust of antiracist whites or Blacks, but get their votes by default).

the lack of political independence by Black Democrats perpetuates their humiliation.

One final "fact" illustrates how brutal the Second Counterrevolution has been on the Black community:

> The number of people in prison, in jail, on parole, and on probation in the U.S. increased by 300% from 1980 [since the election of Ronald Reagan] through 2000, to more than 6 million. The number of people in prison increased from 320,000 to almost two million in the same period. This buildup has targeted the poor, and especially Blacks. In 1999, though Blacks were only 13 percent of the U.S. population, they were 50% of all prison inmates (1 million people). In 2000, one out of three young Black men was either locked up, on probation, or on parole.[21]

This pain and suffering is the product of white supremacy as bipartisan national policy. This material and political reality explains and reinforces the political perspective that Black people in the United States are a nationally oppressed people trapped inside the U.S. nation state. As such, Black people have the right to self-determination, have an independent and conditional relationship to the U.S., and have the right to recourse for their grievances as an "internally oppressed people" in international bodies. This historical and ideological perspective sets the political frame for the events of New Orleans and the Gulf Coast.

The Gulf Coast: The Third Reconstruction (2005 – As Long as it Takes!)

As we turn to proposals for action and remedy, there are Black groups and individuals in New Orleans, the Gulf Coast, and throughout the U.S. who choose to explain their dilemma, their experience, and their demands in a Black-centered, civil rights, antiracist, and self-determination framework. These groups and individuals should be supported by all progressive people, including white people of good will who must stand up to the dominant white supremacy of our times. Let us acknowledge the profound courage required to put forth a perspective based on Black Liberation, which was once the leading view in the Black community. Today, there will be a strong bipartisan "white backlash" against those who think and express themselves in these terms.

These varied forms of Black resistance have already put the Bush Administration and the Democrats on the defensive—if only momentarily. Forced to respond to Black rage—a good example being Kanye West's observation, "George Bush doesn't care about Black people"—Bush, in a mid-September 2005 speech, declared "Poverty has roots in a history of racial discrimination, which cut off generations from the opportunities of America. We have a duty to confront this poverty with bold action."[22] Headlines read, "Bush Talks About Poverty," as if it was a major news scoop that he would talk about race and poverty and even their intersection (which of course it was, and would never be heard coming out of his mouth again).

Still, as we have seen, Bush's neoliberal proposals for "enterprise zones," corporate tax cuts, and his $70 billion corporate giveaway betray his real intentions. Bush's powerfully coded statement that "New Orleans Will Rise Again" is little more than a racist nod to the long-standing Confederate theme "The South Will Rise Again." This ideological and material assault is the challenge to the Gulf Coast and national resistance and to effective plans for a Black-led reconstruction. Yet today, we are not living at a time of a unified Black movement, Black Left, or multiracial movement with a recognized leadership structure that can challenge the political, ideological, and organizational strength of the two-party Right. Without such a counterhegemonic movement, which activists on the ground in New Orleans are working to construct, Bush can transform and pervert generalized acknowledgements of past racial discrimination into a pro-corporate, anti-Black reality.

Grassroots Movements Will Have to Lead—The Democratic Party has Abandoned the Black People of New Orleans and the Gulf Coast.

Every radical social movement needs to build a broad united front to include more moderate and even vacillating allies, and the movement for a Black Reconstruction in New Orleans will need every ally it can get. But the Bush corporate bail-out of New Orleans is both facilitated by the Democratic Party establishment, and the absence of even the most tiny, coherent liberal, antiracist caucus or tendency within the Party. Virtually every white Democrat of any national recognition—from Hillary Clinton to Nancy Pelosi, from Howard Dean to Senate Minority Leader Harry Reid, to former presidential candidates Al Gore and John Kerry, and the opportunist Bill Clinton—has refused to fight against the ongoing civil rights atrocity that is New Orleans and refused to call for an effective Right of Return of more than 250,000 dispersed and abandoned Black New Orleanians.

Many of us had hoped that the Congressional Black Caucus, the self-identified "conscience of the Congress," would provide militant leadership and challenge the Democratic Party establishment and from there the Republicans, but so far little concrete help has been forthcoming. In a seemingly encouraging development, in November 2005, the Congressional Black Caucus introduced the "Hurricane Katrina Recovery, Reclamation, Restoration, Reconstruction, and Reunion Act of 2005—HR 4197" a coherent programmatic plan for the reconstruction of New Orleans from a Black perspective.[23]

On paper it was very encouraging. It has provisions for "A Victim Restoration Fund" and environmental provisions that include "training for responders and clean up workers and public health assessment and monitoring." It also includes a significant increase in stipends for Temporary Assistance to Needy Families, unemployment compensation, health insurance coverage, housing and community rebuilding that includes public housing funds, community development block grants, emergency rental assistance vouchers, prohibition of placement of families in substandard dwelling units, and fair housing enforcement. The list goes on to child care, head start services, relief for elementary and secondary schools, aid for institutions of higher education, voting rights protections, disaster loans and small business relief, and exemptions from bankruptcy restrictions.

On the surface, the Congressional Black Caucus bill is so progressive, so comprehensive, so exciting, that one would have expected it to be a legislative juggernaut to mobilize the Black and progressive communities. *There is only one major problem: the bill does not exist in the real world; it only exists on paper.* So far, the bill has not passed through any Congressional committees in either the House or the Senate, has very few white Democratic co-sponsors, and as we will see, is not even being pushed with any resolve by the Congressional Black Caucus. The bill, like the CBC itself, is trapped inside the white and reactionary-dominated Democratic Party. Tragically, the Congressional Black Caucus often fights only as hard as the white Democratic leadership allows it to.

Glen Ford and Peter Gamble, in their *Black Commentary* article "Katrina: Shock Therapy for Black America," explain how the Congressional Black Caucus has contributed to the Democrats' abandonment of grassroots movements in the Gulf Coast.

> The national Black infrastructure has failed utterly to respond to the Katrina crisis, the wiping out of a majority Black city. The Congressional Black Caucus, which claims to be "the conscience of the Congress" has shown itself to be an appendage of the white [Democratic] House leadership. They slavishly followed Majority Leader Nancy Pelosi's command to make the Democratic Party look good—as opposed to the Republicans—rather than address the crisis that was affecting their own people.
>
> Forty-one of the forty-two Black members of Congress obeyed Pelosi's edict, that the House Committee on

Katrina be boycotted...because it was stacked against the Democratic Party. Of course every committee in Congress is stacked against the minority Democratic Party, that's the way Congress works. But Democrats go to committee meetings every day faced with a Republican majority. Nancy Pelosi, however, was able to convince the Congressional Black Caucus, as a body, to stand down in the face of a horrific crisis, the displacement of hundreds of thousands of residents of New Orleans...

Only Georgia congresswoman Cynthia McKinney broke the Pelosi-invoked boycott [risking retaliation from the Party's House minority leader]. She attended every session, and made good use of the experience, challenging the administration's witnesses every step of the way. The rest of the Black Caucus...failed to make use of the forum in which the New Orleans debacle was being discussed. Why? Because they collectively had nothing to say...They showed their true colors on Iraq, when only Cynthia McKinney out of the whole Black caucus voted for the Murtha bill that called for an immediate exit.

We have a dysfunctional Black Caucus. It cannot cope with the biggest crisis that has befallen our people...ever. A whole Black city wiped off the face of the map. Yet the CBC allows itself to be towing the party line—a white line—based on the logic of a bunch of white consultants who are in search of some mythical white American heartland. That's not where we live. So this is not a commentary about the minutia of legislation that has been introduced under the signatures of various Black congress people. None of it is going anywhere anyway. It is about the failure of Black leadership. We have a dysfunctional Black caucus...drunk on somebody else's power, but it's not ours."[24]

Fighting "Katrina Fatigue"—Supporting Black Leadership at the Grassroots

Given the capitulation of the Democrats, and the crisis of Congressional Black leadership that the *Black Commentator* outlines, the simple but profound realization is that grassroots, Black-led, working class-based labor and community groups must lead the resistance. At this point in history that is easier said than done. The two-party system tries to crush any radical social movements on the ground that would challenge the bankruptcy of the two-party oligopoly. That work is made even more difficult for groups trying to put forth an explicitly pro-Black message. Rev. Lennox Yearwood, chair of the Hip Hop Caucus, in an interview with Damon Azali on the Pacifica radio program *Voices from the Frontlines,* observed that many Black organizations in New Orleans and nationally are being pressured to drop specific references to Black demands, Black liberation, or Black anything. The white backlash in the Congress, for example, threatens to further punish the residents of New Orleans and the Gulf Coast if they put forth any demands that specifically challenge U.S. racism, claiming that such a Black-centered discourse will result in less federal and state funds for the New Orleans relief efforts. Yearwood explained that many Black groups in New Orleans have been pressured to talk more about "all New Orleans residents" or "the poor." He called this white backlash pressure against Black-centered demands "Katrina Fatigue."[25]

Ironically, from the first Black Reconstruction to the present, it has been social movements led by the Black

Left and revolutionary politics that have generated the broadest progressive programs for all working people and for "the poor," including poor and working class whites. Conversely, the liquidation of Black demands has generated reaction and no help for any working people, let alone the poor, and especially the Black poor and working class and the Black community as a whole. The first obligation of a national progressive movement is to support those forces in the Black community who choose to frame their resistance and demand development in terms of Black power, reflected in demands for Reparations, land, and the right of self-determination. The immediate reflection of these politics is the demand for the Right of Return for all 350,000 Black people in New Orleans and the Black community throughout the Gulf Coast at a time when the city is now less than 50 percent of its former population with a massive newly-created Black Diaspora. Only if Black people can get home to New Orleans will there be a social base for a long-term struggle for Black and left power. That single demand, the Right of Return, is the key link to reconstruct a foundation for the people of the Black Belt South.

Today, in New Orleans and the Gulf Coast, there is the historic opportunity to build more unity in the movement and to drive the national and international discourse to the left. Progressive forces throughout the U.S. can offer concrete help to the beleaguered Black community that consistently remains the most progressive force in the country, reflected in a Third Reconstruction from the bottom up. As in the 1960s, when civil rights demonstrators marched in front of establishment targets, the first question of the corporate and governmental flak catchers was "What is it that you people want?" The next section, with its focus on demand development, will offer some answers to that question.

Section II

Notes on a Third Reconstruction: Framing Programmatic Concepts

1. Democratic Rights: Defend and Expand Civil Rights

The struggle for full equality for Black people, to fulfill the rhetorical promises of capitalist democracy, has always been revolutionary in scope. Even the popular radical critique of the U.S. Constitution, that Black people were considered only 3/5 of a human being, gives the system too much credit. It misunderstands the *complete* denial of Black rights that was built into the DNA of the white settler state and the Constitution.

The Constitution, for purposes of representation and taxation, negotiated a compromise between southern and Northern states that was reached during the 1787 United States Constitutional Convention. The so-called "Three-Fifths Compromise" benefitted the Northern states by limiting the power of slave-holding states by reducing their true population; the population of each state was defined as the number of all "free persons" and 3/5 of all "other persons." But this was also a racist reward for slavery in the southern states; since Black slaves were denied the right to vote, the white "free" population of the slave-holding states benefited by wielding the legislative power of 3/5 of the enslaved Black population. Representation and taxation was:

> apportioned among the states according to their respective numbers, which shall be determined by adding to the whole number of free persons, including those bound to service for a term of years, and excluding Indians not taxed, three fifths of all other Persons.[26]

Thus, white supremacy was built into the Founding Father's vision in that even white indentured servants "bound to service for a term of years" were considered "free persons" whereas the Black slaves were permanently, in their view, considered the "other."

The slaves had neither rights nor protections in the Constitution. Slaves were bought and sold as property, they had no civil rights, no right to speak, travel, have a family, or even the right of self-defense to protect themselves from rape, torture, beatings or murder. There were no constitutional provisions prohibiting the mistreatment of slaves, let alone cruel and unusual punishment. This was the premise accepted by both North and South at the official formation of the settler nation as a United States, leaving centuries of long and still unfulfilled struggle for full equality for Black people in this country.

The struggle of the North and South later during the Civil War, the war between whites over the future of the United States, created tremendous opportunities for Black slaves—a parting of the sea if only for a few years. Even before slavery was outlawed by the U.S. Congress, Black people began to overthrow slavery by abandoning the plantation and voting with their feet to join the Union Army at great risk to their lives. "Splits in the ruling class" allowed the Black masses to throw their lot with the North, and in return, win the legal outlawing of slavery.

The right to vote, the right to assembly, the right to own land and to be compensated for centuries of slavery, the right to bear arms (arms they already possessed) the right to live without fear of brutality, abuse, and re-enslavement were central to the early Black Liberation Movement at the end of the Civil War. To their great credit, the Radical Republicans, Black and white, understood the concept of capitalist democracy as a fight for *full and effective* equality between Black and white. These democratic rights had to be protected from discrimination and degradation by the racist practices of an oppressive government, the overt abuses of the growing consolidated monopoly capitalist class, and racist violence by the white masses. The program of the Radical Republicans, including the leadership of Blacks like Frederick Douglass, Robert

Smalls, and two Black U.S. Senators from Mississippi: Hiram Revels and Blanche Bruce, focused on the struggle for complete and compensatory democracy—the early roots of Reparations.

During the 1960s, it was a profound condemnation of the United States that the Civil Rights Movement had a painful sense of déjà vu, "hadn't we already won these rights a century ago?" Or as Melvin Van Peebles sarcastically observed about the mistreatment of Blacks forever and ever: "This can't be America, the land of the free?"

So once again *Brown v. Board of Education* outlawed segregated schools, which had already been outlawed during Reconstruction, and only made "legal" again through the Black Codes, the Jim Crow laws, and the U.S. Supreme Court's racist decision in the case of *Plessey v. Ferguson*, in which the doctrine of "separate but equal" was put forth to justify the most grotesque manifestations of segregation. In 1964, ten years after *Brown*, more than 95 percent of all Black students were still in segregated schools. The Court's gracious admonition to the states that the segregationists should remedy the problem "with all due deliberate speed" meant in practice, "You white folks should eventually end segregation if you ever get around to it." *Brown* was an effort to correct for *Plessey*, and ten years later, the 1964 Civil Rights Act was an effort to create stronger enforcement mechanisms for *Brown*, a court decision with no implementation plans and no consequences for segregationist nullification.

The federal "anti-poverty" programs, the 1965 Voting Rights Act, the important presidential orders against segregation and for affirmative action were all efforts by the Lyndon Johnson administration to break the back of segregation and institutional racism. But like a cancer in the metastatic phase, it was virtually impossible to cure the body of U.S. politics from the disease of white supremacy that was at least 350 years in the making. By the 1968 presidential elections, the Democratic Party, long the party of white supremacy, long the party of the racist Dixiecrats, but lately the party of civil rights, was voted out by the angry, racist, white masses. Just as the Party of Lincoln was overthrown by whites who became Democrats, the party of Kennedy and Johnson was overthrown by whites who became Republicans.

Because democratic rights are not "given," but must be won and upheld and enforced through constant struggle, the racist counter-revolutions have often been successful in overturning legal rights. Today, a Third Reconstruction must begin with the fight for full equality for Black people in the United States. It requires a Third Reconstruction because, in every aspect of U.S. society, Black people are subordinated, discriminated against, subjugated, and denied their democratic right to equality.*

As just one example, the case of *Labor/Community Strategy Center and Bus Riders Union, et al. v. Los*

* The Strategy Center's Program Demand Group has published *Towards a Program of Resistance*, a comprehensive Left program reflected in many of the ideas of *Katrina's Legacy*. The section on Democratic Rights elaborates on this discussion. (*Towards a Program of Resistance*, Program Demand Group, Lian Hurst Mann, editor, Strategy Center Publications, Los Angles, 2001).

Angeles Metropolitan Transportation Authority has become historic—not only because of its civil rights victories but for the role it is playing in the nation-wide struggle over civil rights law. In Los Angeles, California in 1994, the Labor/Community Strategy Center and Bus Riders Union (BRU) initiated a civil rights lawsuit against a $3 billion a year regional agency, the Los Angeles County Metropolitan Transportation Authority (MTA), charging it with establishing a separate and unequal transportation system. The MTA was operating a dilapidated urban bus system for the vast majority of its passengers, who were overwhelmingly Latino, Black, and Asian/Pacific Islander, and a boondoggle high-priced rail system for suburban commuters who were significantly more white as a group, with massive subsidies and state-of-the-art trains. Under Title VI of the 1964 Civil Rights Act, the government cannot discriminate in the use of public funds or services based on race. Represented by the NAACP Legal Defense and Educational Fund, the Strategy Center and Bus Riders Union were able to win a temporary restraining order against the MTA to stop a fare increase and prevent the elimination of the $42 monthly bus pass. Out of that litigation, in 1996, just as the case was finally ready to go to court, the MTA agreed to sign a 10 year Civil Rights Consent Decree with the Strategy Center and BRU, in which we were designated as "class representative" of 400,000 urban bus riders. The MTA pledged to dramatically improve the bus system—promising to reduce fares and maintain the monthly bus pass (which it did), buy more buses, and make the bus system "the priority"—a form of Reparations, or at least compensation for past discrimination. In reality, the MTA never intended to uphold civil rights. It has tried to renege on every promise, has been dishonest, late, and when ordered by the federal district court to finally buy buses for the urban poor of color, has appealed key court orders as high as the Supreme Court.

In this case, the Civil Rights Act has been a great weapon for our movement. Despite the MTA's racist recalcitrance (and yes, with many prominent Black and Latino elected officials on the board contributing to structural racism), the BRU and the federal courts have forced the MTA to get rid of 2,000 filthy, dilapidated diesel buses and replace them with 2,000 brand new Compressed Natural Gas buses, and on top of that, expand the fleet from 2,000 to 2,500. This funding of new buses, drivers and mechanics has required the MTA to invest more than $2 billion, a direct income and service transfer to the urban poor of color. And yet, during the same period, the MTA has still diverted billions of dollars to the rail system, has still raided the bus system for funds to build rail, has still not made bus the priority, and still has practiced policies of separate and unequal—although with a reduction in the inequality. "Reduction in inequality," continuation of racist practices—this is what "victory" looks like in a structurally racist system. Meanwhile, the Clinton and Bush administrations have been appointing judges to the bench who are far more hostile to civil rights, and many of our victories in the courts feel like the last gasps of the end of the civil rights victories of the sixties, the last days of the legal rights won during the Second Reconstruction, co-existing with decades of the systematic dismantling of those rights during the Second Counterrevolution.

The fight for democratic rights always includes a fight against counter-revolution, just as the First Reconstruction had to fight the sabotage of President Andrew Johnson from the first day of Lincoln's assassination. Similarly, precisely because of our great victory in the courts, and the victories of other class action consent decree settlements, Alabama Senator Lamar Alexander has introduced a bill, SB 489, whose supportive material specifically refers to our case as a violation of "government's rights." This bill to "reform" consent decrees is really intended to overturn consent decrees after four years, regardless of their negotiated duration. After four years, contrary to existing law, rather than the burden remaining on the defendants to prove that they have met all the provisions of the decree and thus, should be removed from its obligations, the legal burden would shift to the plaintiffs, to prove that they still need federal protection. Fortunately, as of this writing, this bill has been stuck in the Judiciary Committee, thanks to a broad coalition coordinated by the Leadership Conference on Civil Rights, and some aggressive liberal Democratic opposition. Still, it indicates how the Right does not miss a beat, and will go after the few remaining democratic rights that Black people, as well as Latinos, Asian/Pacific Islanders, and Indigenous peoples have left.

In New Orleans today, the fight for full democratic rights will involve what Du Bois called the "dilemma of Sisyphus," the painful struggle for Black people to carry the boulder of freedom up the mountaintop of racism, only to have the boulder fall down to the ground. This will require the leadership of the most resolute and courageous, to engage a new generation to find the will to fight, and fight again.

The fight for full democratic rights will involve at least the following demands:

- An end to police brutality and the mass incarceration of Black people—the decriminalization of everyday life that will involve a repeal of today's version of the Black Codes;

- Black electoral districts and Black minority guaranteed votes in Congress;

- The extension of the 1965 Voting Rights Act with far stronger provisions against the denial of the full Black vote and over-turning prisoner and ex-prisoner disenfranchisement;

- The release of the vast majority of Black prisoners from Louisiana and U.S. jails and prisons on the grounds that their monumentally high percentage of the prison population is *ipso facto* racism and can only be remedied by overturning their sentences;

- Reparations as a democratic demand, compensation for past centuries of racism to bring actual changes in conditions—jobs, housing, education, income support.

The fight for full democratic rights, which will be elaborated in many of the subsequent sections on demand development, is based on two major theories.

First, that "equality" under the 14th amendment, the "equal protection" clause, is an antiracist principle, and requires a major effort by government to make those who suffer discrimination "whole." That is, by definition those who are not treated equally must receive additional rights and additional benefits to have a chance to catch up with those who benefit from inequality and the denial of rights—that is, the white majority.

Second, those democratic rights must be enforced by the strongest laws with the strongest enforcement mechanisms—civil rights commissions, community review boards for police, fair employment practices laws with criminal penalties for non-compliance. During the First Reconstruction, federal troops were needed to try to enforce the 13th, 14th, and 15th amendments and to protect Black people from Klan violence. During the Second Reconstruction of the 1950s, 1960s and 1970s federal troops were needed to escort children to school in Little Rock and protect James Meredith at the University of Mississippi, and the federal justice department was needed to force recalcitrant states, North and South, to enforce civil rights statutes. The federal courts, through Title VI, which prevents government from discriminating based on race in funding or programs, and Title VII, which prohibits employment discrimination, were essential forces to even begin to remedy almost 500 years of racism as national policy.

Let's be clear—the Republican and Democratic moves towards de-regulation are both an effort to let a "free market economy" go crazy and out of control, but also an effort to "get big government off our backs." This is thinly disguised code to white voters for "get this damn federal government that protects Blacks off our white backs."

The struggle to once again get the police off Black backs and the civil rights laws back on the backs of racist institutions is the core of a new struggle for full democratic rights. Voting rights, immigrant rights, economic rights, rights against unlawful police control, an end to the death penalty, an end to the "war on drugs" altogether, and the decriminalization of drugs—these and many other demands are key to "full democratic rights."

In New Orleans, the Right of Return, so elementary, so revolutionary, requires the federal government to make Black people whole, to restore their previous condition, and if interpreted by a progressive Black movement, given *compensatory* income, housing, and services to make them equal to the white minority.

2. The Right of Self-Determination for Black People in the South and throughout the U.S.

There has long been a debate among Black people about how to define their legal, political, cultural, and governmental relationship to the United States. The various assessments have led to numerous ways to describe and understand this relationship: citizens who suffer from discrimination and who demand civil rights and equal protection of the law; a national minority entitled to special rights based on historical discrimination; an internal colony; an oppressed nation in the Black Belt South with the right of self-determination up to and including the right of secession; an oppressed nation dispersed throughout the United States with a special homeland in the Black Belt South; a people that is subjugated by national oppression and entitled to land, community control, Reparations, and access to international bodies for redress of its grievances. It is not uncommon for many Black people to uphold and identify with more than one of these political categories and strategies depending upon actual historical conditions and the ebbs and flows of their own personal and family experiences.

There also have been comparable and complementary discussions about Black people's relationship to Africa, the peoples and nations of the Third World, other oppressed nationality peoples inside the U.S., and white allies. At times, these formulations have generated enormous energy and clarity inside the Black movement; at other times, these different analyses have generated anger and bitter splits. These differences are both a product of a righteous history of resistance to a common oppression and an effort to generate a very difficult set of tactics, based on the best analysis possible of an oppressed people's situation and options. While a principled struggle for clarity on these questions is called for by the urgency of the historical situation, it is not necessary to have unity on these larger questions in order to agree that Black people in the U.S. have special rights based on their history and oppression that include but also go beyond a legal "equality," requiring restitution, Reparations, land, and self-determination.

In the present situation in New Orleans and the Gulf Coast, the Effective Right of Return becomes the centerpiece of a broad antiracist united front for self-determination. The primary objective is to build broad national and international support for the demands of the beleaguered and strategically pivotal Black community in the United States. The immediate tactical objective is to support those forces in the Black community fighting for the right to self-determination *as a people*, the Right of Return *as a people,* the right to control their destiny in New Orleans and the Gulf Coast *as a people*, and the right to take demands against the United States to the United Nations *as a people.* It is urgent that allies of all nationalities provide support to those groups in the Black community putting forth those views.

The theme of Black self-determination inside the United States dates back to the first African slave on U.S. soil and spans 246 years of slavery and more than 350 years of resistance, including Denmark Vesey, Nat Turner, Sojourner Truth, and Harriet Tubman. It includes the militant abolitionists, the leaders of the First Reconstruction, Marcus Garvey and the "Back to Africa" Universal Negro Improvement Association, the Black communist tradition of Harry Haywood, the African Blood Brotherhood, the cry for "Negro Liberation," and the 1928 and 1930 Resolutions of the Communist International on the Afro-American National Question. It continued through the work of W.E.B. Du Bois and Paul Robeson and their "We Cry Genocide" appeal to the United Nations, SNCC and Muhammad Ali's refusal to fight in the war in Vietnam, Malcolm X's focus on human rights, Black land and separation, rooted in a progressive Black nationalism that reaches out to allies of all races. It extends through Martin Luther King's admonition that Black people in the U.S. must ally with the nations and peoples of the Third World, the Black Panther Party's concept of a Black plebiscite, the Gary Indiana Black Political Convention slogan, "It's Nation Time," and, Randall Robinson's programmatic intervention, *The Debt: What America Owes to Blacks*.[27]

The common and fundamental premise of these past movements and leaders is that *Black people suffered, and still suffer, an egregious, qualitative, and excruciating form of racism, national oppression, and super-exploitation inside the United States (reflected so vividly in New Orleans). As a result, they are entitled to special rights, such as a special status designation that would allow them to bring their collective grievances as a racially oppressed people to the United Nations.*

3. State Unity of the Black Belt South: New Governmental Districts for Black Power

The Black Left during the 1930s apartheid period of the first racist counter-revolution, especially the Communist International represented by Harry Haywood in the Communist Party USA, developed a theoretical position that Black people in the Black Belt South were an "oppressed nation" with the "right of self-determination" in relation to the United States, a separate Afro-American Nation, a Black Nation with the right to secede from the United States. Du Bois also advanced a similar position, especially while writing his ground-breaking book *Black Reconstruction in America*. One of the transitional demands of this Black Nation theory called for the "state unity of the Black Belt

South," in which a newly drawn area of Black majority would form a new unified state structure that had the right to independently determine its relationship to the United States.[28] During the Second Reconstruction period of the 1960s and 1970s, groups such as Malcolm's Organization of Afro-American Unity, the Republic of New Africa, the Congress of African Peoples, and the Black Panther Party continued the ideological tradition calling for Black self-determination and, for some, Black states in the South. This view had considerable influence during the 1960s in a more revolutionary context, but still, recently resurfaced during the 2000 and 2004 George W. Bush presidential "victories." This view was reflected in widespread Black opposition to the segregationist role of the electoral college system and the stealing of Black votes in the South.

The "state unity" analysis and strategy—instead of trapping Blacks inside majority white states and using the "winner take all" electoral college (which has led to the white population taking all)—calls for a unified bloc of Black majority states with one coherent Black governmental body. For example, such an area could unify all the Black majority counties in the South, moving across current state lines to create new governmental districts that would be Black majority and Black governed. Another version of this idea calls for the creation of a series of new Black majority states, which could ally as a federation in the South to directly challenge white power.

From Marcus Garvey's "Back to Africa Movement" to Malcolm X's charge that Black people should take their national demands for land and self-determination to the United Nations to the Black Panthers' discussion of a Black plebiscite, the concept of a Black nation has influenced the ideology of many leading thinkers, even if actualization seemed difficult to achieve. And while support for the Black Nation perspective has ebbed and flowed depending on the strength of the movement, shorter term and transitional demands, such as the fight for majority Black electoral districts (most of which ultimately have been overturned by the Supreme Court), have consistently generated broader support.

The New Orleans story raises many questions about political power. What forms of political power can Black people in the South exercise if they are trapped inside white majority states? What is the future of 20 million Black people in the South who, in state after state, are outvoted by racist white majorities and the Electoral College system? Despite their massive total vote—for which generations risked and gave their lives—the effective Black vote is systematically diluted and sabotaged. As Bob Wing documented in his article "White Power in the 2000 Election":

> The Electoral College negates the votes of almost half of all people of color. For example, 53% of all Blacks live in the Southern States, where this year (2000), as usual, they voted 90% Democratic. However, white Republicans out-voted them in every Southern state (and every border state except Maryland). As a result, every single Southern Electoral College vote was awarded to Bush. While, nationally, whites voted 54-42 for Bush, Southern whites, as usual, gave over 70% of their votes to him. They thus completely erased the massive Southern Black (and Latino and Native American) vote for Gore in that region.[29]

How to rectify this grim situation? There is a programmatic discussion that focuses on Black people demanding sovereignty and the right of self-determination in their own areas of population majority and finding ways to leverage their 20 million votes against the national political system. At the very least, the demand to rebuild New Orleans as the Black city it was before the human-made hurricane, based on the Right of Return, could be an important step in this process.

There were also proposed reforms in the Electoral College system to allow for proportional representation. For example, Harvard Law School Professor Lani Guinier has stressed the importance of Black majority electoral districts, though her nomination to the Justice Department was jettisoned by Bill Clinton when white racists in Congress labeled her the "quota queen." Still, taking these arguments to their logical conclusion suggests redrawing racial boundaries in the South (and North) to create Black majority Congressional districts and Black majority states, to free Black people from mandatory white-majority rule.

4. Reparations: The Debt America Owes to Blacks

> It would behoove African Americans to remember that history forgets, first, those who forget themselves.[30]
>
> *Randall Robinson, The Debt: What America Owes to Blacks*

In his book, *The Debt: What America Owes to Blacks*, Randall Robinson calls for comprehensive Reparations to the Black community. The former director of TransAfrica

Forum, Robinson argues that the U.S. must account for the crimes of the Trans-Atlantic Slave Trade, the deaths of 25 million Africans en route, and centuries of slavery and Jim Crow apartheid. With regard to remedy, Robinson is clear that the solution must be massive and carried out over many generations to redress more than 246 years of slavery, and more than another 140 years of sharecropping, peonage, and now mass imprisonment. He calls for comprehensive social programs that begin with a legal admission of guilt by the United States government and corporations, a finding that would have legal standing in U.S. courts, international courts, and the court of public opinion. Robinson's pioneering book asserts that the demand for Reparations is not a one shot deal or a separate issue but rather an integral part of reshaping the civil rights, antiracist, and Black Liberation movements. This analysis calls for a material assessment of the egregious psychological, cultural, and material suffering that Black people have endured, a crime against humanity that has lasted for centuries and continues to exist to this day. Consequently, the remedies must be massive, encompass *all* Black people, with a particular focus on the Black poor, and be implemented for decades until full and compensatory justice is achieved.

As Robinson explains:

> American capitalism, which starts each child where its parents left off, is not a fair system. This is particularly the case for African Americans, whose general starting points have been rearmost in our society because of slavery and its long racialist aftermath.[31]

Robinson's initial thoughts on the scope of the remedy can help reframe today's debate in New Orleans—as well as the struggles in New York, Houston, Los Angeles, Detroit, Atlanta, and every other major city, town, and area of the country.

Robinson continues:

> With respect to the question of compensation to African Americans, it has been proposed by Robert Westley, in "Many Billions Gone,"[32] that a private trust be established for the benefit of all African Americans. The trust would be funded out of the general revenues of the United States to support programs designed to accomplish "the educational and economic empowerment of the trust beneficiaries (African Americans) to be determined on the basis of need"...I believe that such a trust would have to be funded for at least two successive generations, perhaps longer. Among other programs funded from the trust would be special K-12 schools throughout the United States with residential facilities for those black children who are found to be at risk in unhealthy family and neighborhood environments. The curricula for these schools would be rigorous, with course requirements for English, advanced mathematics, the sciences and foreign languages. Additionally, the schools would emphasize the diverse histories and cultures of the black world...Further, all blacks who qualified academically and were found to be in financial need would be entitled to attend college free of charge.
>
> On the private side, a study funded by the trust would be undertaken to determine the extent to which American and foreign companies or the existing successors to such companies, or individuals, families, and public institutions, were unjustly enriched by the uncompensated labor of slaves or by the *de jure* racial discrimination that succeeded slavery. Compensation would then be sought from those

> companies, institutions, and individuals—and fought for with the same vigor that Under-secretary of State Stuart Eizenstat demonstrated on behalf of Jewish survivors of the Nazi holocaust, inducing sixteen German companies under pressure from the U.S. to establish a fund of 1.7 billion dollars to compensate mainly Jews used as slave laborers during the Nazi era.[33]

At the 2001 World Conference Against Racism in Durban, South Africa, there were days of the most moving and intellectually advanced discussions of how and why the nations of Europe and the United States owed Reparations to the nations of Africa, to Black people in the U.S. and to all of those in the African Diaspora. One area of consensus was that Reparations for crimes against humanity should be the basic frame that shapes both the comprehensive and massive settlement of claims and present-day demands—for example, freeing all Black prisoners to remedy the explicitly racist criminal justice system, demanding "Jobs or Income Now" for all Black people, and a massive government fund for Black people, to be administered over at least a 50-year period, that would provide income support, housing, and land (the modern version of the oft-promised but never delivered 40 acres and a mule).[34]

In the New Orleans context, the argument for Reparations could be integrated into a coherent set of demands that addresses the racism of the actual hurricane planning, relief, and rebuilding efforts. Reparations demands could require concrete remedy to George Bush's epiphany that poverty is "rooted in generations of racial discrimination" (based on broadcast images of 150,000 stranded and drowning Black people on every TV set in the world). Saladin Muhammad of Black Workers for Justice observed that when delegates returned from the World Conference Against Racism, there was enthusiasm about a campaign to make a series of Reparations-centered antiracist demands on the U.S. government. However, that momentum was crushed by the events of September 11, 2001, less than a week after most of us in the U.S. delegation returned from South Africa. The New Orleans and Gulf Coast movement now has the chance to rescue the victories of WCAR by making Reparations for Black people in the U.S., the peoples of Africa, and all those in the African Diaspora a strategic frame and component of their demands.[35]

Specifically, a Black united front in the Gulf Coast could call for federal aid to Black communities that would bypass the Federal Emergency Management Agency (FEMA) and the Office of Homeland Security. Instead, these funds could go directly to grassroots movements with social programs conceptualized as part of the broader movement for Reparations—such as programs to organize Black collective land, parks, hospitals, farmers cooperatives, and rehabilitation centers for released prisoners.

Another critical Reparations demand would focus on land. The U.S. government could use its powers of eminent domain to secure land from corporate forces and wealthy white individuals and to distribute land to a new generation of Black farmers and a new generation of Black urban dwellers—by whom land would be collectively and cooperatively owned.

By 1910, despite widespread fraud, theft, and forcible confiscation by white bandits, nearly one million Black farmers in the U.S. owned a total of 15 million acres; today, there are fewer than 18,000 Black farmers, representing less than one percent of all farms and owning less than one million acres.[36] This is impacted by the growth and consolidation of agribusiness and the destruction of "family farming" in general, but as with all general trends, the consequences come down on Black people like a ton of bricks. For almost a century and a half, since the formal abolition of slavery, Black people have been driven off their land and dispersed, with little or no income, to cities all over the United States. The story of how the federal government, corporate agribusiness, and white vulture farmers conspired to steal and embezzle land from Black farmers—using fraud, beatings and murder, often with the full involvement or acquiescence of local "law enforcement officials" and the federal government—is almost too painful to remember, let alone tell.

Congressman William Lacy Clay (D-MO) has observed:

> The wholesale theft of land from African Americans is the greatest unpunished crime in our nation's sordid history of race relations. Land ownership was the ladder to respectability and prosperity in the Old South—the primary means to building economic security and passing wealth on to the next generation. So when Black families lost their land, they lost everything. Typically, Blacks were forced off their lands with phony charges of non-payment of taxes or through claims of counter-ownership by other private or government entities. In other cases, African Americans were forced off their lands with threats of violence or the outright murder of Black landowners.[37]

Today's movement could demand that the federal government, as part of the more than $70 billion allocated for the Gulf Coast "rebuilding plan," secure a substantial area of prize farm land to be given free to Black farmers willing to till it, and even more land for Black farmers willing to create large-scale agricultural co-ops. Because there is virtually no way today for small farmers to compete with the ruthless Wal-Marts of agribusiness (firms such as Cargill and Archer Daniels Midland), the federal government should provide guaranteed markets and guaranteed contracts and profits for Black farms. This could be achieved through government procurement contracts with Black farmers to supply food to government agencies, food stamp programs, and expanded income-support programs for New Orleans and U.S. residents. This could guarantee commodity prices and cost-plus contracts for Black farmers instead of guaranteed profits for Halliburton and Bechtel. It could also take place at the same time as lifting all agricultural subsidies for U.S. monopoly agribusinesses that dump subsidized farm products in Third world countries.

In addition, the demand for land has profound application to urban dwellers in major cities as well. Publicly and cooperatively owned land needs to be developed to address the particular public and cooperative housing needs of Black residents who rent. The present concentration of most Black people, and most people in the world, is now in large urban centers, such as the greater New Orleans area. Thus, Black demands for land will have to address urban, as well as rural land—low-income housing, collectively owned land for parks and recreation, land for urban schools with campuses, land for urban gardens and housing cooperatives.

Black demands for land need not be subject to prior property claims or proof of prior ownership by individuals, but, rather, should be based on a collective demand of an oppressed people seeking redress and Reparations. After all, if slavery and almost 150 years of post-slavery governmental racism and national oppression have denied an entire people—Black people—life, liberty, and the pursuit of happiness, stolen their labor and stolen their land, then the level of compensation must go beyond private property laws that reward theft, to human rights laws that demand redress and Reparations for past crimes.

5. The Right of Return and the Resettlement of Black Evacuees

The central tactical demand that has united the Black and progressive movements in New Orleans, the Gulf Coast, and throughout the United States and that has given that movement its cutting edge, is the Effective Right of Return of 350,000 Black residents of New Orleans and comparable numbers in every other Gulf Coast city.* If the Black population of evacuees is not aided in its return, there can be no material base for Black power and no political base to challenge the racist institutions in New Orleans, the white,

* The term "right of return" has been initiated by the Palestinian people who were forcibly expelled from their land by the Israeli government and army. The self-conception of the Black movement as a "Third World" movement, and concrete solidarity with the dispersed Palestinians, and now Lebanese people, has never been more relevant or urgent.

anti-Black majority in Louisiana, the U.S. Congress, and the anti-Black President. Areas of Black majority are critical to any possible reversal of policies that contribute to racism and national oppression. They must be fought for and defended as if all of our lives depended on it.

Without a plan to prioritize the return of Black people to New Orleans, relocation has taken the form of mass kidnapping and the forced dispersal of refugees.

As Beverly Wright of the Deep South Center for Environmental Justice observed shortly after Katrina:

> We need to go beyond the 'Right of Return' to the 'effective Right of Return.' We need plane tickets, bus tickets, housing, and a job or at least government benefits waiting for us when we do return. We cannot allow the Bush Administration and even many Louisiana white Democrats to support the forced and conscious dispersal of Black New Orleans and Gulf Coast evacuees to 'new homes' in Houston, Boston, Los Angeles, and Utah that effectively cements their disenfranchisement. They must, every one of them, be allowed to return home![38]

New Orleans has never been a large city. At its height, the population was about 600,000 people and by the 2000 Census it was down to less than 500,000 people, almost 350,000 of whom are Black. Already the policy to evacuate the city and institute a state of massive dislocation—without coherent plans to return all residents after the flooding—has created systematic Black removal. The Bush Administration was guilty of criminal negligence in the evacuation of the vulnerable. Now, the two-party system is guilty of sabotaging their repatriation. As of this writing, our worst fears have been realized. Almost a year after Katrina, New Orleans is a city of no more than 200,000 people, of whom perhaps 50 percent are Black—a loss of at least 250,000 dispersed black residents since Katrina struck!

A worst-case scenario for Black New Orleans residents is already happening. A massive construction project is underway to address the engineering problems of a city below sea level, but it is reflected in government bailouts and pork barrel projects for the corporate elite. The poorest Black sections, currently uninhabitable, will take years to rebuild, and yet, people who want to rebuild are being refused that right. Meanwhile, many of the most affluent white residents already have basic services and will create the core of the new population. Bush claims that New Orleans will "rise again," but who will live in it and who will reap the benefits of the rebuilding process? Will it be those who suffered the pain of the hurricane? Or will New Orleans be "whitewashed," the goal of many for years?

When the rebuilding is completed, new and improved, many affluent whites will be attracted to move in at rents and home purchase prices much higher than what low-income people can afford. A *Los Angeles Times* article, "Speculators rushing in as the Water Recedes," by David Streitfield describes the crimes of gentrification and land speculation.

> The land rush has long-term implications in a city where many of the poorest residents were flooded out [and 84% of all those classified as 'poor' are Black]. It raises the question of what sort of housing—if any, will be available to those without a six-figure salary.[39]

New white, affluent settlers will make demands for more police, gated communities, and just enough Black and Latino people to work in Wal-Mart and sweatshops, and to clean homes and hotel rooms—a majority white city with a low-wage Black and Latino working class.

What Beverly Wright, Saladin Muhammad, and many Gulf Coast organizers predicted is materializing as a worst case scenario. Unless a unified movement can reverse the trend—the *white-ification* of New Orleans will continue to move full speed ahead.

Such a movement to challenge this racist redevelopment plan is already in motion. The People's Hurricane Relief Fund is demanding that the federal government "provide funds for all displaced families to be reunited." The fight for a Black Reconstruction must involve the guarantee that New Orleans will be rebuilt as a Black majority city and returned to its pre-Katrina population of 500,000. This will involve a thoughtful debate about a future urban plan for the city that must go beyond rebuilding the levees and waiting for the next hurricane season. It will require a multiracial movement with strong, progressives Black leadership to put forth a plan to Reconstruct New Orleans from the bottom up.[40]

6. Katrina was an Environmental Injustice: Environmental Justice Must Shape Reconstruction

> We are long past the point where global warming is considered a myth. We are seeing its effects all around us, especially in my hometown of New Orleans, Louisiana, which is expected

> to experience an increased incidence of flooding that could potentially destabilize its economy and endanger its populace. We must be realistic about long-term solutions to global warming [by] reducing carbon emissions for the future benefit of African Americans and all U.S. citizens.[41]
>
> *Rep. William Jefferson, (D-LA) 2004*

> Category Five Hurricanes are a rare breed. Since records have been taken, less than five percent of all hurricanes have gone on to be Cat Five storms. However, in just the past two seasons, the Atlantic Basin has had two such storms, Isabel and Ivan...hurricanes at its maximum level of intensity and extreme destructive power—with sustained winds of more than 155 miles per hour.[42]
>
> *Hurricane News 2004*

The catastrophe in New Orleans is human-made. There are at least four interrelated reasons to place the blame at the feet of "the system," a.k.a. U.S. imperialism.

First, global warming is a relatively recent, human-made disaster, the product of 100 years of the most intense escalation of the number of autos on the planet, an increase in high horsepower supercharged engines, and failure on the part of world governments, most specifically the U.S., to address the problems of fossil fuel and chemicals driving the economy and to take the radical, revolutionary steps required to reverse it.

Second, cities have developed in a way so that the most vulnerable populations—the poor, Indigenous communities, and communities of color—are situated in the most dangerous areas, and are denied transportation, food, and the resources to survive or escape. The entire idea of "regulating capital," which is the least radical proposal, is under attack by an out-of-control business elite.

Third, the evangelical, right-wing movement is attacking the very basis of scientific inquiry and knowledge as a guide for public policy. As the system deteriorates materially, intellectually, and spiritually, a religious fanaticism based on Christian evangelism is exuding a ferocious anti-scientific bias. This madness is undermining even the "rational capitalists" who do not support social justice but do not want the system itself, or its major cities, to fall apart at the seams. As the scientific proof of global warming is becoming incontrovertible, the religious Right and the Bush Administration are putting forth the fairy tales of "creationism," "intelligent design," and a Biblical apocalyptic vision of a sin-driven Armageddon to explain the flooding and the deaths. According to this right-wing worldview, an angry Christian god wreaking his retribution is raised to the level of truth, while the devastating impacts of fossil fuels, a car-crazy society, and Western greed and disregard for the planet are attacked as falsehoods. The history of the failed efforts to develop a long term and ecologically viable plan for New Orleans in the decades before "The Big One" during which other hurricanes had long since exposed the vulnerability of the city itself is another reflection that U.S. capitalism is in its dying stages as a civilization.

Fourth, the political system of the white settler state will not fight for the lives of Black people. This is in sharp contrast to the urgency and decisiveness exhibited towards white, affluent communities facing similar threats, e.g. the Northridge, California earthquake after which FEMA came in like Santa Claus and moved decisively and generously to compensate all who were impacted. In fact, combined with the attacks on the social safety net, as well as on programs for regulating environmental impacts, these differential impacts are qualitative, class-driven, and racist.

Extreme Weather Events—One Face of Global Warming

Why was Hurricane Katrina "the worst natural disaster in U.S. history?" Why has it happened now? At the Strategy Center we learned through our participation in the World Summit on Sustainable Development in Johannesburg, South Africa that one of the key reflections of the destructive impacts of global warming is what the Alliance of Small Island States calls "extreme weather events." The climate change crisis already affects many Third World countries. The documentary film, *Rising Waters: Global Warming and the Fate of the Pacific Islands*,[43] illustrates that nations and peoples that have anticipated and controlled flooding for thousands of years are now experiencing uncontrollable super-sized floods, hurricanes, and tornados. Island and coastal nations and peoples in the Third World who previously had effective mechanisms to protect themselves from terrible but predictable weather events are now overwhelmed. Coral reefs, which have functioned as natural levees to protect against flooding, are being destroyed by warmer ocean temperatures. Torrential winds, rains, and floods go beyond "normal" terror, and yet the system tries to pawn these off as natural disasters. Indeed, they are human-made disasters. As Ronald Brownstein observed in the *Los Angeles Times*:

> Last month in the journal *Nature*, Kerry Emanuel, professor of atmospheric science at MIT and author of the new book *Divine Wind: The History and Science of Hurricanes*, examined the intensity of hurricanes in the North Atlantic and western Pacific oceans since the 1930s. The total amount of energy the hurricanes released—a figure calculated from wind speed and duration—"has increased over the last 50 years by somewhere between 50 percent and 80 percent," he said. "That is a whopping big increase. And it is very well correlated with tropical ocean temperatures."
>
> In a recent article in the journal *Science*, Peter J. Webster of the Georgia Institute of Technology and three colleagues reached a similar conclusion with different data. These researchers found that the share of hurricanes around the world reaching the most intense categories (4 or 5 on the Saffir-Simpson scale) was almost twice as large in the past 15 years as from 1975 through 1989. Only one-fifth of hurricanes reached those peak intensities in the earlier period, the researchers found, compared with 35% since 1990.
>
> Just as important, the researchers concluded these changes had occurred "in all of the ocean basins"... Released last year by NOAA's Geophysical Fluid Dynamics Laboratory, the study concluded that "greenhouse-gas-induced warming may lead to a gradually increasing risk in the occurrence of highly destructive Category 5 storms."[44]

Enele Sopoaga, Ambassador and Permanent Representative to the United Nations of the island nation of Tuvalu, explains that the Alliance of Small Island States, with forty-four member island countries in the Pacific, in the Caribbean, in the Indian Ocean regions, and some in the South and Western African continent, is particularly concerned that the U.S. contributes about 25 percent of the carbon dioxide greenhouse gas emissions into the atmosphere yet will not agree to the Kyoto Accords.

> The Alliance addresses the vulnerability of small island countries against, particularly, climate change. Any slight increase in the level of the sea will seriously affect the livelihood of the people living on islands. The scientists have predicted that over the next fifty years, the level of the sea could rise up to 2.9 meters, which is quite, quite big for an island country which is hardly three meters above sea level. These disastrous economic, social, and environmental impacts are not limited to the small island states, but will continue to pose a major threat to those who live near the seacoasts throughout the world.[45]

Dr. Paul Epstein, from Harvard's School of Public Health, points out that Third World countries in particular are vulnerable to epidemics provoked by global warming because they already lack secure housing, medical services, and nutritional and medical care.[46] Such man-made death and destruction is exemplified by the impact of a Category Five Hurricane on decaying cities with vulnerable populations in the United States as well.

Barry Commoner, the reknowned biologist, has argued that the development of massive horsepower cars, the proliferation of diesel and other fossil fuel-based power, and the use of chemicals to solve problems previously resolved without ecological intrusions has qualitatively increased toxic emissions since World War II to a level greater than during the entire history of the world combined.

The auto, oil, and highway industries contribute to the production of greenhouse gases that generate global warming and climate change, which in turn cause the extreme weather events, which in turn are imposed on vulnerable peoples resulting in their illness, dislocation, homelessness, despondency, and death. Entire communities, mostly poor and of color, are destroyed. At the time of the 2004 Indian Ocean tsunami, the most deadly earthquake and flood in recorded history, several Third World commentators observed that we should not simply say the tsunami killed between 170,000 to 250,000 people, but rather 170,000 to 250,000 "poor people." Except for some unfortunate tourists, it was the poorest of the native populations who absorbed most of the blows—those who received no warning, those who could not evacuate, those without resources, those already sick and hungry, and those living in the most vulnerable areas. *Throughout the world, it is the Black, Latino, Asian/Pacific Islander, and Indigenous peoples who are the human sacrifices to the Western god of profit.*

With regard to the specifics of New Orleans, Brian Azcona and Jason Neville, graduates of New Orleans colleges and universities, have published a post-Katrina paper titled, "Unnatural Disaster: Louisiana's Crisis in Policy and Planning."[47] While many have focused on the fragile condition of the levees, the under-funding of levee repair, and the fiasco of the Bush dismantling of FEMA, these authors focus on how the destruction of the wetlands through corporate development agendas undermined one of nature's ways of mitigating the impact of hurricanes:

> President Carter created FEMA in 1979 to address the country's worst-case disaster scenarios and New Orleans has consistently been on the top of that list. In 1995, the International Panel on Climate Change of the United Nations identified New Orleans as the most vulnerable North American city to global climate change, because of

> sea-level rise and elevating temperatures on the Gulf of Mexico intensify the frequency and power of hurricanes... In the last century, over 1.2 million acres of land have disappeared, in large part as a consequence of land misuse—that includes oil, gas, and timber extraction; industrial, commercial, agricultural, and residential development.
>
> These economic activities required destructive modifications to the coastal areas such as erosive canals, levees, and drainage systems. Historically, these coast wetlands provided invaluable flood protection by acting as a sponge to soak-up the menace of the storm surge. Where land once stood is now open water...Economic development reduced the absorbent capacity of the region, while simultaneously increasing runoff and toxicity.[48]

A climate justice perspective would begin with demanding regulation of the corporations, laws that restrict the "individual choice" to pollute, mandated increases in auto fuel efficiency, reduction in auto use and dramatic toxic use reduction, expansion of public transportation, and the community's "right to know" the chemicals and greenhouse gases produced by corporations and institutions.*

Translating this sentiment into action and program could begin by proposing that New Orleans be reconstructed as an "auto-free city," that is, a city with many auto-free zones, auto-free days, auto-free rush hours, and other forms of

---

* Since this was written, we received an environmental justice report and analysis, "In the Wake of the Storm: Environment, Race, and Disaster After Katrina," written by long-time EJ and social justice scholars Manuel Pastor, Robert Bullard, James Boyce, Alice Fothergill, Rachel Morello-Frosch, and Beverly Wright, and published by the Russell Sage Foundation. It is available at www.russellsage.org. We urge readers to download and read this important article.

restricted auto use. The vision: a massive, federally-funded, clean-fuel bus, jitney, bicycle and pedestrian-centered free, public transportation system to rebuild New Orleans in a way to reduce the danger of global warming and combat transit racism. This perspective would also demand dramatic reductions in emissions from Louisiana's oil refineries in Cancer Alley, the 85-mile stretch on I-10 between New Orleans and Baton Rouge, as well as the grain elevators and steel plants. It would call for a moratorium on highway expansion, the preservation of wetlands, and a moratorium on coastal development, beginning with a complete moratorium on gambling boats coming inland to set up coastal enclaves.

A Black Reconstruction in its most progressive manifestation would see itself as part of a multiracial movement for environmental justice to propose the unthinkable: cities in which people, particularly low-income Black people, and not the auto, oil, highway, and chemical industries, are prioritized.*

---

* Many of these ideas on sustainable urban development have been developed in considerable specificity by the Labor/Community Strategy Center and Bus Riders Union (BRU) and are already, after more than a decade of work, reflected on the streets of Los Angeles. The BRU has forced the Los Angeles County Metropolitan Transportation Authority, through a civil rights Consent Decree signed with the MTA in 1996, to improve its bus service. The collaboration between the LCSC, BRU, and NAACP Legal Defense and Educational Fund has forced the MTA to put 2,000 Compressed Natural Gas buses on the road, retiring most of its dilapidated diesel buses, and to expand bus operations by another 500 buses. The BRU has won significant reductions in bus fares, stabilized bus fares for nearly a decade, improved overcrowded conditions on the buses, and dramatically expanded student bus pass distribution and bus ridership itself. The BRU has generated a comprehensive New Service Plan that prioritizes transporting the transit-dependent, and eventually all Angelenos, to jobs, medical centers, and educational facilities. The BRU is currently demanding that the MTA and new L.A. Mayor

7. Black Women in the Eye of the Storm

The focus on the Black community in New Orleans also requires a focus on the specific oppression and strategic role that women play in the post-Katrina battle for reconstruction. It also requires analysis and specific programmatic demands to address the needs of low-income, working class Black women, as a critical force within the entire multiracial women's movement, the entire Black movement, and the worldwide united front against racism and imperialism.

The Institute for Women's Policy Research (IWPR) has published a comprehensive report, "Women of Gulf Coast Key to Rebuilding After Katrina and Rita:"

> Women of New Orleans and the Gulf Coast are especially hard hit by hurricanes Katrina and Rita as they are more likely than men to be in poverty, to head single-parent families...Of all families with related children under 18, female-headed families make up 56% in the city of New Orleans, compared to 25% for the nation as a whole. Many of these families also live below the poverty line. Four in ten female-headed families in New Orleans are poor...median earnings for African-American women

---

Antonio Villaraigosa implement "bus-only lanes" on major urban thoroughfares to prioritize the bus over the auto, so that bus service can be faster for the transit dependent, and also convince "choice riders" to get out of their cars. Copies of the Consent Decree, articles on this work and two strategic papers that describe the outlook—*A New Vision for Urban Transportation* and *An Environmental Justice Strategy for Transportation in Atlanta: The View from Los Angeles*—as well as the *BRU Five-Year Plan for Countywide New Bus Service*, can be found at www.thestrategycenter.org and www.busridersuion.org.

> who worked full-time, year round were quite low in all of the regions hit by the hurricanes, with the city of New Orleans at $19,951...[49]

The historic racism of the white South has caused enormous suffering for all poor people, especially the Black poor. The white majority's efforts to subjugate Black people is compounded by the most severe cases of male supremacy and institutional misogyny. All of this hatred against Black people, Black women, women, and the poor is fundamentally rooted in plantation politics. This history of white male privilege creates the ideological vindictiveness that justifies abominable social welfare policies. As the IWPR's "Status of Women in the States" report observes:

> Louisiana, Mississippi, and Texas all rank in the bottom ten of all states on a number of indicators of women's status... On women's poverty, Texas ranked 44th, Louisiana ranked 47th, and Mississippi ranked last in the nation. These states also ranked in the bottom of all states for health insurance among women.[50]

Joni Seager, writing in the *Chicago Tribune*, presented an historical assessment of how "natural disasters expose gender divides:"[51]

> As the media coverage of the disaster in New Orleans swung into high gear, reporters [saw] that the dead, the dying, and the desperate on the streets of New Orleans were African American...This disaster fell hard on one side of the gender line too. Most of the survivors are women. Women with children, women on their own, elderly women in wheelchairs, women everywhere—by a proportion that

> looks to be somewhere about 75 to 80 percent...Disaster is seldom gender neutral. In the 1995 Kobe, Japan earthquake, 1.5 times more women died than men; in the 2004 Southeast Asia tsunami, death rates for women across the region averaged three to four times that of men.[52]

Moreover, underfunded, dysfunctional, or even non-existent public transportation systems overlay and reinforce gender oppression.

> In the days ahead of the storm, a lot of people did get out of New Orleans, almost all of them by car. Poverty combines with ideologies about gender to provide deep disadvantages in terms of mobility. Even in a country as awash in cars as the United States, women are less likely to have a car or a driver's license than their male counterparts. Of all Americans, it is poor women who are least likely of all to have a car or access to it.[53]

We have seen this in our own organizing work with the Bus Riders Union in Los Angeles. The bus system is 85 percent Black, Latino, and Asian/Pacific Islander, but on most inner city routes, the bus ridership is virtually 100 percent oppressed nationality peoples. The median family income of bus riders is $12,000 a year, and almost 60 percent of the riders are women. Again, the class, race, and gender dynamics are usually reflected in the same human being, as virtually 60 percent of all bus riders are working class, very low-income, Black, Latino, and Asian/Pacific Islander women. Those women would be the most isolated and abandoned in an L.A. earthquake just as in a New Orleans hurricane.

As described in the section on Reparations, the destruction caused by Hurricane Katrina has provided an opportunity to go beyond asking to restore things to how they were before, because what existed prior to Katrina was already unbearable. Today, we have an opportunity to dramatically expand the entire framework of social services for families, women, and children—slashed since the Reagan 1980s and compounded by Clinton's cynical move to "end welfare as we know it."

Loretta Ross, the National Coordinator of Sister Song, elaborated some important demands in her paper, "A Feminist Perspective on Katrina,"[54] beginning with increases in centers for women's health and abortion provision. "Mississippi already had only one abortion provider before the storm. Women traveled to Louisiana or Alabama for services. What will an already-underserved region do to help women receive reproductive health care?"

As Chief Justice John Roberts managed to be confirmed without making his view clear on abortion rights (although his track record leaves little doubt about his misogynistic intentions) and Justice Samuel Alito is a ferocious opponent of women's rights to abortion, the demand for a new network of abortion and reproductive health care centers throughout the South and the Gulf States would raise consciousness and provide material aid to women in need. This would combine the demand for a woman's right to choose with the urgent economic and social reality of working class women. For poor women, children having children is such a repetitive cycle that many young women are changing diapers before they have had a chance to wonder what they would want their own life to be like. While the factors in the "cycle of poverty" are complex and cumulative, the right of low-income women, who are overwhelmingly Black, to defend the integrity of their own bodies, reflected in access to birth control, protection against forced sterilization and the right to government-funded safe abortions, is a critical component of the solution.

One gendered component of the demand for jobs or income is to prevent women and children from being forced into prostitution. In the present militarized framework of disaster relief, a progressive program must demand a zero-tolerance policy for U.S. soldiers and military bases in the Gulf Coast creating centers of U.S. government procured prostitution rings.

As Loretta Ross explains with regard to Gulf Coast redevelopment:

> Often poor women and children are the first ones forced into prostitution to survive. There will be an increase in the demand for prostitution created by the massive military and police presence in the affected states, similar to the rise in prostitution that surrounds our military bases around the world already. Women are not "opportunities to relieve stress" as many soldiers are encouraged to believe. Because of the limited real choices women face, we expect there will be a rise in the prostitution and trafficking of women and children, and the exploitation and sexual abuse of displaced children—generating unwanted pregnancies, sexually transmitted diseases, and HIV/AIDS.[56]

A Comprehensive Safety Net for Women

Ross ends with programmatic suggestions that are comprehensive in scope:

> We can use this moment to force bureaucracies to be more flexible, like changing normal admissions procedures to get our kids back in schools or demanding that quality public housing be provided instead of permanent refugee camps. We need schools, voter registration, immigrant services, drivers licenses, housing, medical care, and public assistance put on the fast track, not bottle-neck services mired down in typical bureaucratic snarls that characterize government assistance services.[57]

The core of the demands presented above is that for centuries, the poor, and especially low-income Black women, have been warehoused in government programs that are only one step above the poor house and the debtors prisons that preceded them. During the 1960s, there was a major change in public policy and public attitude towards the poor, and Black women in particular. A new generation of social workers and county employees actually believed the government and "the system" were responsible for poverty and that government programs could be part of a "war on poverty" that named poverty itself, not the poor, as the enemy. Women's reproductive rights were respected as part of national policy, and a vibrant women's liberation movement forced those issues onto the national agenda.

Today, women's right to abortion has been demonized by a racist, women-hating Right Wing driven by the desire to put women "back in their place," that is, white women subordinated to men in the nuclear family, and women of color subjugated to superexploitation and hyper-oppression by imperialism—U.S. imperialism in particular. The demands of low-income Black women in the Gulf Coast for social welfare programs, an end to government encouraged prostitution, and full reproductive rights aggressively defended by men in a revitalized Black community and progressive movement, are critical building blocks of a Third Reconstruction.

8. No to the Police State! Yes to the Social Welfare State!

The responsibility of the State to govern leads it to be a contested terrain, especially under bourgeois democracy. While the government of a nation with a capitalist economic system will, for the most part, be run by representatives of the capitalist ruling class, nonetheless, the tactical promise of democracy makes possible an arena of political struggle for broad democratic rights, curbs on capitalism's abuses and the government's repression, and a social safety net. Even under capitalism's constant drive for accumulation, a contest remains between a social welfare state and a corporate welfare state, popular control of bourgeois democracy or executive control of a fascist police state. As the centuries long fight for basic civil rights has shown, the fight for a Third Reconstruction in the Gulf Coast is another such arena of contestation over control of state power.

Disaster Relief Must be Demilitarized

In the first days of Katrina, the TV shots of Black people in groups without food or water, with signs reading "Help me," and with no assistance for days pulled at the heartstrings of people throughout the world. But when "help" finally arrived, it was in the form of police, national guards, and soldiers of the U.S. Army. The arrival of the police state is not what is needed. Even as Black people were fighting to survive, Louisiana Governor Kathleen Blanco, a Democrat, announced the arrival of 300 "battle-tested" Arkansas National Guard troops fresh from service in Iraq. Blanco warned, "They have M-16s that are locked and loaded. These troops know how to shoot to kill and I expect they will."[58]

The Bush Administration has used the mantra of "September 11" to further expand its police state plan. All disaster relief has been placed under the jurisdiction of the Office of Homeland Security (OHS), although nothing military was needed to rescue people and provide flood and humanitarian relief. Rather than sending massive aid in the name of FEMA (already under OHS control) President Bush at first considered sending federal troops into Louisiana by citing the "Insurrection Act," which authorizes the federal government to unilaterally bring troops into a state to quell revolts despite the objections of the state government. The fact that no such insurrection was taking place or the consideration that if Black people did rise in insurrection they should be supported rather than attacked was outside the realm of the two-party debate. The Democratic governor clearly objected to a reduction in her authority, and Bush eventually rejected the option, knowing that the Republicans cannot be seen as challenging the white supremacist ideology of state's rights. Since then, all emergency measures have been totally militarized. The fact that the federal government was slow to activate its resources is criminally negligent, but that does not mean that next time we want a more rapid *military* occupation, or for that matter, any military presence at all.

This will involve dismantling the bogus Office of Homeland Security or, at the very least, excluding natural and human-made disasters from its jurisdiction. The Black community and the Left could call for the reconstruction of a Civilian Conservation Corps and, as long-time labor and Black liberation organizer Bill Fletcher suggests, the recreation of the Works Progress Administration program that was so effective during the Great Depression.

In the immediate Gulf Coast context, it is critical to demand both an end to state violence and police abuse as well as the creation of new civilian agencies on the spot.

Yes to the Social Welfare State!

The concept of "jobs or income now," raised by the Communist Party USA during the Great Depression, and raised again by Dr. Martin Luther King Jr. in preparation for his 1968 Poor Peoples' Campaign, includes the demand for a "social wage" by means of which the government supplements the incomes of low-income people (and the entire society) by providing a full range of government services that support individuals, families, and communities.

The Office of Economic Opportunity (OEO), "The Poverty Program" initiated in 1964, responded to some of those demands, and, to the degree that they were implemented, Black income and conditions of life improved (as did those of the white poor). Within a few short years, the OEO's "community action programs" based on the progressive concept of "the maximum feasible participation of the poor" led to creative community organizing in every major city, marked by Black-led protests against corporations, landlords, and racist government programs. Since the cities were the stronghold of the Democrats, this often led to direct confrontations with Democratic mayors who tried to buy off the most opportunist community leaders and repress those who were un-bought and un-bossed. Frightened by the rise of grassroots organizing and the reality of the maximum feasible participation of the poor, the Democratic big city mayors finally asked Congress to dismantle the community action components. The Democratic congress obliged, passing the Green Amendment in 1977 that closed down community action programs and transferred all power and funds back to city hall. This effectively dismantled the anti-poverty program just as it was getting off the ground.[59] The positive result? It led a new generation of Black, Latino, Asian Pacific Islander, Native American, and antiracist white organizers to further reject the Democrats and turn to revolutionary politics.

Thus, today in New Orleans, there is no need to recreate the failed attempt at "U.S. government-inspected" community organizing. But the perspectives of Jobs or Income Now is critical to shape today's debate. There is no way a capitalist, profit-driven market (now codified in popular bourgeois ideology to the point it is personified as "The Market") can provide enough living wage jobs for the army of Black poor that existed before Katrina, let alone the growing army of those who must return. Only by re-energizing the mass demands for economic rights and the social wage/income supports, full employment, government as employer of last resort, renter's credits and new public housing, full medical benefits and public hospitals—can the Black poor, and low-income working class people of all races, win the battle of ideas as the critical first step in winning the battle for political and economic power.

A coherent and comprehensive long-term social-service program should, at the least, include the following:

- *Jobs or income now.* An income support program is urgently needed. If all 350,000 Black people in New Orleans received, at a minimum, $10,000 each, it would only cost $3.5 billion per year, $17.5 billion over five years. If those benefits were extended, as they should be, to all working class, displaced people including poor whites, that number would only be $4 billion a year—while the entire aid package already approved for New Orleans is now upwards of $70 billion. Direct stipends are the most cost-effective way to bring funds to Black and low-income residents, who, in turn, can support Black and area businesses through their purchases.

- *A newly-built public housing system.* Because the massive high-rise, post-World War II, public housing experiments were never developed with the resources and maintenance budgets that high-rise housing requires, they have been broadly criticized, while the Right (and most liberals) have conveniently abandoned the concept of public housing altogether. The much vaunted "Section 8" private sector solution—through which low-income people get rent credits and private landlords reap the benefits while renters never get to own—only reach a tiny percentage of those in need and can only be a secondary element of the solution. If new landlords get massive government subsidies to construct brand new buildings, they will not want to rent to the poor, and especially the Black poor, whether they are subsidized or not—since decent apartments and houses are now renting and selling at inflated prices that will drive out many former residents. Low-rise, decentralized public housing units, including mixed income housing developments, must be prioritized in the plan.

• *Increased social services.* Head Start programs, mental health services, and new public hospitals and community clinics also create new public sector jobs at truly livable wages. The expanded social sector with government guaranteed high wages is a key component to a reconstruction effort.

• *Prevailing wages in all public projects.* It is mind-boggling that George Bush would dare to unilaterally remove the "prevailing wage" provisions of the Davis-Bacon Act, passed in 1931. This at the same time that he is practically handing over "no bid, cost overrun" contracts to corporate parasites such as Bechtel, Fluor, the Shaw Group, and Halliburton. That means that no matter how much the companies charge the government, they are not even required to pay $9 per hour, which is the typical "union wage." Grassroots groups can demand that the

Democrats force Republicans to abide by the prevailing wage provisions in all federal contracts in Louisiana and the Gulf Coast.

• *Affirmative action in all federal contracts, including access by non-union labor.* This will require that Davis-Bacon is not used as a front for white racist union practices. For many of us who have mechanically repeated "Don't repeal the Davis-Bacon Act," few of us know that the origins of the 1931 act were to prevent Blacks from being hired on federal contracts. Lily-white and racist labor unions wanted to protect "union" (that is, white) jobs from Black competition—while keeping Blacks out of the unions. Thus, the demand for prevailing wages must be combined with demands for affirmative action, including hiring Black people at least in their proportion of the overall pre-Katrina population. It is the responsibility of trade unions in New Orleans, Louisiana, the South, and throughout the U.S., both AFL-CIO and Change to Win unions, to place the fight for civil rights at the front lines of any class-based demands: *Black people from New Orleans, regardless of union affiliation or lack thereof, must be hired on all federal projects at least consistent with their percentage in the population—that is, at least 67 percent of all federal jobs.*

Fighting Enterprise Zones and a Post-Katrina Capitalist Make-over of the City

Movement demands on the private sector are also critical for a Reconstruction in New Orleans—from high-wage jobs to corporate clean-ups and reductions in pollution to affirmative action hiring at all levels for Black people, women, and all people of color.

The work of a broad coalition of grassroots groups in New Orleans is critical to provide a programmatic challenge to the corporate private and corporate public "make-over/take over" of New Orleans that, if not challenged, will further oppress and marginalize the Black poor and working class. If the Bush/Democratic Party master plan, still to be negotiated but already moving full-speed ahead, is not met with powerful resistance, corporate-oriented "community" and clergy forces tied to the Republican and Democratic parties will cut deals, get their piece of the action, and once again abandon the fundamental needs of the community as a whole, especially the Black poor.

In Los Angeles, after the 1992 urban rebellion, L.A. Mayor Tom Bradley and right-wing California Governor Pete Wilson colluded to reject massive public funds for the Black and Latino poor and, instead, trumpeted a "private sector" renaissance. This was at a time when "the market" was promoted throughout the world as the rational force to clean up the failures of the socialist experiments. They tapped Peter Ueberroth, the former head of the L.A. Olympic Committee and Commissioner of Baseball, to lead a private sector "investment-based" fiasco called "Rebuild Los Angeles." Some groups in the Black community bought into the plan's false promises that massive private investment would be forthcoming and would lead to more jobs and higher income.[60]

In reality, sectors of the Black and Latino communities tied to the church, corporate, university, and Democratic Party hierarchies, abandoned demands for guaranteed government jobs for urgently needed public infrastructure, massive social services, environmental justice protections, and restrictions on police brutality. Instead, they agreed to the deregulation of the corporations, the lowering of corporate taxes, the easing of already-inadequate environmental standards, and the creation of so-called "enterprise zones" in which employers could pay lower wages. This system of free-market chaos and deception was all held together with an increase in the police force, selling its occupation of communities in the name of "community-based policing," the very same LAPD (but then with a Black police chief, Willie Williams) whose brutality had generated the L.A. rebellion in the first place.

Two of the most pernicious effects of the brief Rebuild L.A. private sector "market" euphoria were the undermining of community demands on government and corporations for jobs and social services, and the generation of an ugly competition among the most opportunist forces in every oppressed nationality community for seats on the Rebuild L.A. board. Tremendous tensions between Black and Latino corporate-oriented community leaders led to fighting over funds and jobs that did not even exist and private investment that was never coming. By the time Ueberroth exited Rebuild L.A. and snuck out of town under cover of night, the possibility of a public sector social, welfare state movement had been killed, while the private sector solution never existed, let alone materialized.

During that period, from 1992-1993, the Labor/Community Strategy Center formed the Urban Strategies Group, and published *A Plan to Defeat the Federal Weed and Seed Program in Los Angeles.*[61] Weed and Seed was a federal Justice Department program that would have set up special enforcement zones in Black and Latino communities where more severe federal laws would supersede state laws. In coalition with AGENDA (Action for Grassroots Empowerment & Neighborhood Alternatives) and other community groups, the Strategy Center helped to build a coalition that actually got the L.A. City Council to reject federal funds for the Weed and Seed program. The Strategy Center then published *Reconstructing Los Angeles, and U.S. Cities, from the Bottom Up*, challenging the private sector myths of Rebuild L.A. and offering an alternative reconstruction plan for Los Angeles.[62] Through a year of organizing and broad coalitional united front work, we created a significant and well-publicized counter-force to the combined Democratic/Republican/corporate oligarchy. In many arenas, including the establishment media, we won the ideological fight over the future of development in Los Angeles—if only in the immediate post-rebellion aftermath. We were not strong enough to beat back the actual economic march of de-regulated capital, but we were able to pursue a movement building strategy that won many community groups away from the false promises of the private sector siren.

This corporate-driven development plan is repeating itself in New Orleans. As post Katrina events have brutally clarified, there is a new, unelected, behind the scenes, ruling class oligarchy running the city. This cabal can disregard the fig leaf of local government because Mayor Nagin and the New Orleans City Council has virtually no independent political clout of its own. It must depend upon alliances with Baton Rouge and Washington. As Mike Davis explained in the *Nation Magazine*:

> While elected black officials protested from the sidelines, a largely white elite has wrested control of how to rebuild the city. The *de facto* ruling cabal includes Jim Amoss, editor of the New Orleans *Times Picayune*; Pres Kabacoff, developer-gentrifier and local patron of New Urbanism, Donald Bollinger, shipyard owner and prominent Bushite, James Reiss, real estate investor and chair of the Regional Transit Authority (i.e. the man responsible for the buses that didn't evacuate people); Alden McDonald Jr. CEO of one of the largest black-owned banks; Janet Howard of the Bureau of Government Research (originally established by the Uptown elites to oppose the populism of Huey Long) and Scott Cowen, the aggressively ambitious president of Tulane University.
>
> But the dominating figure and kingpin is Joseph Canizaro, a wealthy property owner who is a leading Bush supporter. He is also the power behind the throne of Mayor Ray Nagin, a nominal Democrat (he supported Bush in 2000). Finally, as the former president of the Urban Land Institute, Canizaro mobilizes the support of some of the nation's most powerful developers and prestigious master planners....As Canizaro told the *Associated Press* last October, "As a practical matter, these poor folks don't have the resources to go back to our city, just like they didn't have the resources to get out of our city. So we won't get all those folks back. That's just a fact."[63]

Or, as they say, "the wish is the father of the act."

So what does the new downtown elite want the future of New Orleans to be? Just what every movement activist in New Orleans has known for decades:

> For years, Reiss, Kabacoff, and others have complained that New Orleans has too many poor people. Faced with dire fiscal consequences of white flight to the suburbs, as well as three decades of de-industrialization...they argue that the real interests of underemployed African Americans might be better served by a Greyhound ticket to another town.[64]

From the first days of Katrina, Black activists understood the story only too well. The Black majority would be forced out permanently, would never get home, and the city would have a smaller and whiter footprint—if the movement did not stop them. This new plan for downtown corporate development is already in place, and the bipartisan conspiracy has been out in the open for all eyes to see since the first drops of rain and the first gusts of wind.

But no one, even with the most clear minded and radical critique, could have anticipated the extent of the system's criminal attacks on the Black poor, those remaining in the city, and those in the Diaspora still planning to come home.

A policy of free enterprise zones and homesteading acts is diverting billions of public funds into private, corporate coffers as corporate welfare. At best, a few thousand community residents are benefitting while structural aid to the 350,000 member Black community in New Orleans is being undermined.

We hear that Bush has allocated $70 billion for New Orleans and the Gulf Coast, but we now know that most of those funds are being used for the rebuilding of corporate areas by corporate parasites, and worse, it is really being financed by more than $40 billion in cuts of social services. Bush and the Democrats must be pressured to reverse their plan whereby the private/corporate sector raids public tax funds to ensure guaranteed profits.

The counterhegemonic alternative? Repeal the reduction and phasing out of the inheritance tax; raise the taxable levels of the highest incoming-earning 20 percent of the population; stop any cuts in social security benefits or eligibility; cut the $400 billion military budget by at least 10 percent a year ($40 billion available just next year alone) until it is reduced to below $100 billion and deprived of any first-strike and offensive capability, and immediately withdraw the imperial occupation of Iraq, freeing up hundreds of billions of dollars and, more importantly, freeing the Iraqi people and the U.S. troops sent to fight and die for interests that are not their own.

The battle between the public sector and the private sector—and the battle within the public sector between social services and the police state is in the final analysis, a fight over the capitalist state itself, its composition, its class politics, and the power of conflicting classes and races. That race and class struggle frames not just the future of New Orleans but the future for all of us.

9. Free the Prisoners

Louisiana has the notorious distinction of being the "prison capital" of the United States. Although Louisiana's population is only about 4.5 million, it has incarcerated 51,458 people in its state prisons, federal prisons, and local jails (June 2005 data). This is at a rate higher than the reactionary state of California, which has 246,317 inmates out of a population of 36 million (June 2005 data). In fact, Louisiana has the highest incarceration rate in the country, with 1.1% of its population incarcerated (1,138 prison and jail inmates per 100,000 residents in 2005).[65a] There are 5,100 prisoners alone in the maximum-security Angola Prison, which is located 60 miles northeast of Baton Rouge (named for the incarceration of so many former slaves who were originally from the African nation of Angola). This is also the largest prison in the United States and among the most notoriously brutal. It is estimated that 85 percent of the prisoners in Angola Prison will die there; 75 percent of the prisoners are Black, even though Blacks comprise only 32 percent of Louisiana's total population.

The fight in Louisiana has to challenge U.S. national policy as well, in that the United States is the world's largest jailer.

> Nearly seven million adults were in U.S. prisons, or on probation or parole at the end of 2004, 30 percent more than in 1995, the Justice Department said. Whites represented 56 percent of the probation population and only 34 percent of the prison population, while Hispanics make up 12 percent of the probation population and 19 percent of the prison population, and Blacks represent 30 percent of probationers and 41 percent of prisoners...The total number of people incarcerated in the U.S. grew 1.9 percent in 2004 to 2,267,787 people.[65b]

The 13th Amendment—Freeing the Slaves and Setting the Legal Trap for Their Re-Enslavement

The 13th Amendment to the U.S. Constitution was a breakthrough in the legal prohibition of slavery and set the constitutional grounds for "freeing" the slaves. Unfortunately, it also created the legal grounds for their re-incarceration and re-enslavement. The entire amendment reads as follows:

> Section 1. Neither slavery nor involuntary servitude, except as a punishment for crime whereof the party shall have been duly convicted, shall exist within the United States, or any place subject to their jurisdiction.
>
> Section 2. Congress shall have power to enforce this article by appropriate legislation.

For years, civil rights scholars and Black people of every class looked to the 13th Amendment with gratitude and awe—for it did outlaw "slavery and involuntary servitude." Even with all the disgraceful backsliding of white people, formal slavery was still abolished—allowing for greater options for the Black movements in the North and South to continue the fight against the First Counterrevolution. It took still another century of struggle, but many of the institutions of re-enslavement, such as sharecropping, poll taxes, the Black Codes, and the night riding of the Klan, have been dramatically scaled back by the courage of the civil rights movement.

But racism against Blacks as a people is endemic and intractable in U.S. culture. Prohibited and beaten back in one form, racism, like a mutated virus, reappears in a new disguise, a new form. Who today would know that the 13th Amendment had a provision so that slaves freed out the front door could be re-imprisoned through the back door—the U.S. prison system. Contrary to how it is represented, the 13th Amendment does not outlaw slavery and involuntary servitude altogether. It outlaws them, "except as a punishment for a crime whereof the party shall be duly convicted." This isn't in the fine print at the bottom of the contract, it is right up there in the first sentence of the amendment.

In fact, the 13th Amendment can't even give the abolition of slavery its own sentence. "Neither slavery nor involuntary servitude" can't even connect with "shall exist within the United States" before it is interrupted by "except as a punishment of a crime whereof the party shall have been duly convicted." Going to jail is put right into the heart of the 13th Amendment, and in fact, is even given more words.

So let's be clear, from the outset, the freeing of the slaves and the locking up of Black prisoners were two sides of the same coin. By 1866, the Black Codes were passed by defiant southern state legislatures. They set into motion the criminalization of everyday Black life. The Black Codes and normal southern white practice allowed the local sheriffs to pick up Blacks on the corner for "loitering," lock them up, and send them to work for local white planters. At virtually the same time as the passage of this amendment, the Ku Klux Klan was formed in 1868, with the support and participation of the majority of white southerners. While Blacks celebrated the end of centuries of the most abominable slavery, the majority of white people intened to re-enslave and re-imprison the Black population—and yes, generate chain gangs and indentured farm laborers in cahoots with the white farmers large and small. This *Racist Re-Enslavement Complex* was an integral part of white cultural formation—an intersection of the super-exploitation of Black labor and state and public terrorism that has defined white settler culture from its inception until today.

During the "two decades of the sixties," including the election of many genuinely liberal and decent Democrats and even the now extinct "moderate Republicans" the country moved away, if only for a moment, from its punitive, racist roots. Widespread discussion of poverty, racism, and multi-racial camaraderie became popular among a significant part of the population, and for a moment, a cultural revolution took place among a significant number of Blacks, Latinos, Asians, Indigenous peoples, and whites that put the Right temporarily back on its heels. In the 1960s few prosecutors asked for the death penalty, and between 1967 and 1972 there were no executions anywhere in the United States. In 1972 the U.S. Supreme Court even abolished capital punishment, but almost to punctuate the end of the "two decades of the sixties" in 1975, by 1976 a more conservative Supreme Court reinstated the legality of the death penalty.

In 1980, Ronald Reagan was elected president, and the Second Counterrevolution formally began, with its attacks on "welfare queens" and its calls to punish the protestors that had violated the norms of patriarchy, white supremacy, U.S. world domination, and the culture of white Christian vindictiveness. Reagan promised to put the masters' house back in order, and he kept his campaign promise: Let the massive expansion of police, arrests, and prisons begin. The result: the astronomical rise in the U.S. prison population from 300,000 in 1980 to more than 2.2 million people today—with more than 1 million Black and 500,000 Latino prisoners. The Racist Re-Enslavement Complex is one of the most pernicious and defining aspects of the Second Counterrevolution.

How do we explain the profound vindictiveness in white-majority culture against Blacks that goes far beyond economic roots and the drive to maximize profits and super-exploit labor? The great orator and abolitionist, Frederick Douglass, as a child, had a master who was known as a "slave breaker." For more than a year, he beat Douglass every day and barely fed him, forcing him into a temporary breakdown that few individuals could have survived. Miraculously, Douglass, and many other slaves, were able to transform a living hell into a strategy for liberation and a humanizing culture in the midst of degradation. The psychic "wages of whiteness" (that Du Bois brought into the lexicon of antiracist thought) begin with white privilege, the plantation economy, and the northern segregated suburbs, then mutate into the myth of white superiority and are further transformed into a white blood lust—a hatred of Blacks, Latino immigrants, Arabs and foreigners. The white aggressors do not see themselves in this light, of course. Rather, they feel constantly under attack. For them, the Blacks are the aggressors and they are the victims—which leads to, "lock them up and throw away the key" or "execute them all." (The classic picture of a crowd of several hundred whites in the South during the 1930s, including many children, having a celebration as they laugh and point to the body of a hanged Black man on a tree is an eerie reflection of this phenomenon.)

During the First and Second Reconstructions many white people have encountered their greatest nightmare—the angry, militant, and armed Black man poised to pay them back for their sins. For centuries, used to running plantations where they controlled every movement of slaves by armed force, transforming the countryside into an armed white camp and corralling northern Blacks into urban ghettos presided over by armed police forces, the white majority, frightened by the possibility of a Black and Brown majority, is now in a state of racist panic. They use their ill gotten gains from a system of white supremacy to portray themselves as the "law abiding" good people. They vote early and often to imprison youth with "adult" sentences, call for "3 strikes and you're out," vote for more prisons, more police, and more prisons again and again. They vote to make each sentence longer and longer, while cutting funding for the public defender's office, hating any amendments that protect people's rights (after all, if you weren't guilty why would you need them?) They watch Court TV, Fox News, CNN, and 30 "Law and Order" episodes a month in which their worldview is reinforced.

This form of sado-imperialism is reflected in the abuses at MyLai, at Abu Ghraib, in the murder of 24 civilians in Haditha, Iraq and in the U.S. missiles helping Israel saturation bomb Lebanon and its civilian population. The analytical frame of "sado-imperialism" can best explain why there are more than one million Black people in prison—and why the Black male calls himself "an endangered species."

The Racist Re-Enslavement Complex is central to the First and Second Counterrevolutions.

Ironically, it is the exception that proves the rule. Throughout the United States there are millions of white people who actively reject institutional racism. They work as teachers in inner city schools, as social workers and psychologists, as public defenders and civil rights attorneys. They are militant union members and clergy, and conscious, northern and southern civil rights workers. And they are disproportionately Jewish, a people with a long history of experiencing racism, pogroms, torture, demonization, degradation of their physical and cultural characteristics, concentration camps and genocide. This allows many Jews to deeply identify with the Black experience and the Black struggle.

Decent white people who are true friends of the Black community, of Latinos, of immigrants, of gays and lesbians, are subjected to a special hatred by the racist Christian white majority so that now even the word "liberal" has become a conservative, racist epithet. During the height of the civil rights movement, there was an unmitigated hatred of white civil rights workers by the white racists—nothing compared with the hatred directed toward Blacks, but frightening nonetheless. *Today, there is a need for another civil war among whites*—in which white antiracists, as part of a multiracial Left, stand up for Black and Latino rights, for immigrant rights, and take on the white, Christian, evangelical Right. Many are already doing so; many more are needed.

The concept of the Racist Re-Enslavement Complex helps us better understand the mass incarceration of Black people for the crime of being Black, and ties it to the complex workings of a capitalist, imperialist system. In 1865, there were four million Black slaves. Today, there are more than a million Black people in prison. If we include Black parolees and those awaiting trial or sentencing, and include their family members whose lives are directly hurt by this mass incarceration, the number extends to more than five million Black people.

A recent report, "Race and Incarceration in the United States" by Human Rights Watch,[66] reveals the continuing, extraordinary magnitude of minority incarceration and the stark disparity in their rates of incarceration compared to those of whites. Out of a total population of 1,976,019 incarcerated in adult facilities, 1,239,946 or 63 percent are Black or Latino, though these two groups constitute only 25 percent of the national population. The figures also demonstrate significant differences among the states in the extent of racial disparities.

Among their findings on the incarceration of Blacks:

• In 12 states, 10 to 15 percent of adult Black men are incarcerated.

• In 10 states, 5 to 10 percent of Black adults are incarcerated.

• In 12 states, Black men are incarcerated at rates 12 to 16 times greater than those of white men.

• In 15 states, Black women are incarcerated at rates 10 to 35 times greater than those of white women.

• In 6 states, Black youth under age 18 are incarcerated in adult facilities at rates 12 to 25 times greater than those of white youth.

> Blacks have also been disproportionately affected by the national "war on drugs", carried out primarily through the arrest, prosecution and imprisonment of street level drug offenders from inner city communities. In 1996, for example, blacks constituted 62.6 percent of all drug offenders admitted to state prisons. In at least fifteen states, black men were sent to prison on drug charges at rates ranging from twenty to fifty-seven times those of white men. Blacks are prosecuted in federal courts more frequently than whites for crack cocaine offenses, and thus as a group have felt the effects of the longer sentences for crack versus powder cocaine mandated in federal law. Racial profiling and other forms of unequal treatment of minorities by the criminal justice system have further contributed to the over representation of minorities in the incarcerated population. Minority youth are treated far more harshly compared to similarly situated white counterparts within the juvenile criminal justice system.
>
> Some of the greatest racial disparities in rates of incarceration occur in states in which minorities are concentrated in urban areas.[67]

The Reagan election in 1980 formally started the Second Counterrevolution, with his Secretary of Education, the compulsive gambler William Bennett's, "war on drugs" campaign that directly resulted in the massive incarceration and re-enslavement of Black youth. In 2006, after Katrina, Bennett said, "If we wanted to reduce the crime rate we could abort all Black babies." (While he tried to qualify the statement by saying that such a decision would be immoral, he had already scored the point, and the suggestion was well understood by his audience. He could have simply continued with, "Well, if you find that idea too extreme, just continue the logic of my war on drugs and we will eventually lock up most of them anyway.")

The Mass Re-incarceration and Re-enslavement of the Black Nation

There are nine million prisoners in the world, of which 2.2 million are in the United States. The U.S., with five percent of the world's population, has 24 percent of the world's prisoners. Usually, an imperial homeland would have less prisons and prisoners, saving its most cruel and barbaric practices for its colonies, "protectorates" and spheres of influence in the Third World. But because the United States has a "Third World within," it chooses to inflict similar punishments, especially on the Black and Latino peoples who live inside its borders.

In Louisiana, mistreatment of the victims of Katrina was amplified by the conditions of the prisoners who are on the chain gangs at Angola Prison, to those on death row, to those youth incarcerated for the most minor, petty, and punitive criminal laws (e.g., the "war on drugs") that are causing an epidemic of imprisonment in the Black community. Many Black prisoners, after being incarcerated for three to seven years, are released with just $10 in cash, no place to stay, and no job. They are disenfranchised, not allowed to vote because they are designated as ex-felons, and are often quickly rounded up for the most minor and often bogus infractions of probation and parole and are then sent back to the living hell of prison.

The extraordinary demands needed to address the New Orleans crisis should include releasing most of the prisoners in Louisiana, treating those remaining with rehabilitation and dignity, and launching a national campaign to care for the urban and rural poor in every major city in the country.

"Prisoners' Rights" in the Midst of the Storm

In the early weeks after Hurricane Katrina, Human Rights Watch and Families and Friends of Louisiana's Incarcerated Children (FFLIC) unearthed another of the attendant horrors of the Katrina disaster—the abandonment, near drowning, possible drowning, and 519 missing inmates from Orleans Parish Prison compound.

> As Hurricane Katrina began pounding New Orleans, the sheriff's department abandoned hundreds of inmates imprisoned in the city's jail, Human Rights Watch said today. Inmates in Templeman III, one of several buildings in the Orleans Parish Prison compound, reported that as of Monday, August 29, there were no correctional officers in the building, which held more than 600 inmates. These inmates, including some who were locked in ground-floor cells, were not evacuated until Thursday, September 1, four days after flood waters in the jail reached chest level. "They

> left us there to die," said Dan Bright, an Orleans Parish prisoner...Many of the men held in jail had been arrested for offenses like criminal trespassing, public drunkenness, or disorderly conduct.[69]

To build public support for the plight of abandoned and possibly-drowned prisoners requires challenging the ideology of racism and the punitive public posture that are the bedrock of the mass incarceration machine and the mass hysteria against prisoners. The exposé that prisoners were abandoned must compete with the outrage felt about those abandoned at the Superdome and those who are dispersed with no funds or jobs. The concept of 519 prisoners unaccounted for will generate, among conservatives, the spectre of a "mass jailbreak" rather than the plight of human beings, most of them caught up in a system of mass incarceration of the poor and the Black. This excellent investigative and organizing work of FFLIC and Human Rights Watch led to the firing of the New Orleans police superintendent "because of the department's horrific performance in the Katrina disaster." *The New York Times* editorial section called on the city to "scrutinize correction officials and the officers who work for them."[70]

In the past months since the Orleans Parish Prison scandals, a new coalition on prison reform has been built—Safe Streets/Strong Communities, a coalition that includes FFLIC, Fairness for Prisoners' Families, A Fighting Chance, Juvenile Justice Project of Louisiana, Southern Center for Human Rights, and Voices of the Ex-Offender (VOTE). Their platform, includes important proposals to reform the

New Orleans Police Department, reform the Orleans Parish Prison system; reform the New Orleans Criminal Justice Court system, including to "build, expand, and prioritize alternatives to incarceration."[71]

This is the challenge of what is called "counterhegemonic organizing"—raising demands that challenge the structures and the ideology of the existing system. How do you go beyond disciplining and firing the most sadistic and incompetent prison guards and officials (or just those who happen to get caught), to challenge the existence of the prison system and the entire criminal injustice system? How do you go beyond punishing those who brutalized and abandoned the prisoners to freeing most of those young men, almost all of whom are Black. They should not have been in prison in the first place because of the systematic racism, discrimination, and national oppression reflected in the entire criminal injustice system. This is compounded by the "war on drugs" and the unspoken war on Blacks based on the criminalization of every day life—from drunk and disorderly conduct, drug possession, loitering, and all the other behaviors that white middle and upper-income people can carry out with impunity.

The Black community is suffering mass unemployment, their growing exclusion from the low-wage and working class economy, the massive police and now National Security State, compounded by a widespread deep political depression, reflected in "A Raisin in the Sun." This is the product of 25 years of the Second Counterrevolution, now on the verge of escalating into the First Mass Fascism of this period, resulting in a Black community under siege.

This is now happening at the same time that the system is moving to criminalize more than 12 million immigrants in the Latino community, using "immigration reform" to build a police state in the form of the Office of Homeland Security and Immigrant Customs Enforcement (ICE), which has helped send more than 500,000 Latinos to prison, many for drug and immigration infractions, neither of which should be illegal in the first place.

Today, the grotesque behavior of the the prison officials in Angola and Orleans Parish Prison has created the opening and opportunity for a prisoners' rights movement and raise more fundamental demands against the Louisiana prison system based on the de-carceration, that is, the freeing of prisoners en masse, and the repeal of most criminal statutes. The fight for the humane treatment of prisoners and the removal of incompetents, sadists, and racists from positions of authority are critical first steps, but they become even more effective, as partial and reform demands, if they are accompanied by more systematic and fundamental ones—such as mass release of Black prisoners, Reparations, land, and self-determination. "Free the prisoners, put the real criminal on trial," "Free the U.S. 2 million," "Let our children come home," "Stop the Attacks on the Black Family," "Stop the Black Codes," "Get your hands off me," "Listen Up School Board: I want to be pre-med, pre-law, pre-job, not pre-prison," and the famous immigrant rights chant, "No human being is illegal," can help "free the prisoners" and include them among those who deserve a new opportunity and a new franchise in the "land of the thief and the home of the slave."

10. Immigrant Rights and Native Rights Are Part of the Third Reconstruction

The growing Latino population in the South is an important new ally for the Black community. A Black/Latino alliance is critical to challenging rightward shifts by both the Democrats and the Republicans. But that will be very difficult to achieve.

Many of us in the civil rights and Black liberation movements of the 1950s, 1960s, and 1970s witnessed the strategic and moral leadership of the Black movement in encouraging liberation movements in the Latino, Indigenous, Asia/Pacific Islander communities, and mobilizing millions of antiracist whites to their cause. Indeed, Native American activists and Latino militants learned from the Black Power movement and were encouraged to initiate their own struggles for land and self-determination, leading to "strategic alliances" between "Third World" peoples internationally and inside the U.S. For example, Fan the Flames: A Revolutionary Position on the Chicano National Question, written by the August Twenty-Ninth Movement (ML), declared:

> Looking back at the '60s we can see that the Afro-American liberation movement gave inspiration and impetus to all other progressive movements in this country. The slogans, demands and tactics of Afro-Americans, were adapted in varying degrees to the struggles of Puerto Ricans, Native-Americans, Chicanos, students, women, veterans, and the working class.
>
> Particularly would the Afro-American struggle in the Black Belt South be affected by a Chicano national revolt.

> Two great peoples, whose nations border in part, united by their oppression and their struggle, living in the heartland of their enemy. Both with revolutionary histories, with the thread of armed resistance running throughout; both with a growing and militant working class, toiling in the major strategic industries of their enemy. No one can deny the galvanizing effect that armed land seizures by the Chicanos would have on the Afro-American people in the south.[72]

Within the progressive and left sectors of the Black community at the national level, there have been voices crying out for a Black/Latino alliance and even support for the rights of undocumented workers. Bill Fletcher, a veteran of the labor and Black movements, has appealed to Black activists and the Left with the challenge: "How can we forget about the tragedy of how Katrina has impacted undocumented workers as we fight to protect and defend the Black community?"[73]

Glen Ford of the Black Commentator, in an editorial "The Insanity of Black Anti-Immigrant Politics," observed,

> It is quite upsetting to see Black legislators making common cause with the most racist elements of the Democratic and Republican parties, in proposing draconian measures to criminalize those who are undocumented...who somehow believe there is political profit in allying Blacks with nativist whites—who actively agitate against Black interests, as well as those of Latinos. This is insane...
>
> The greatest political challenge facing Blacks in the urban centers is to find common ground with Latinos...in the common need for employment at a living wage and the struggle against gentrification...The driving forces behind

> criminalizing Latino immigrants are the same ones that have criminalized whole Black communities, and created an African American Gulag in the nation's prisons.
>
> African Americans have a stake in influencing the political behavior of Latino immigrants, with whom we must negotiate for control of the cities. We know who the enemy is—the same one who brought us to this country in chains, who is also the same one who stole half of Mexico.[74]

Saladin Muhammad of Black Workers for Justice has called for a coherent Black/Brown alliance of the Black Belt South and the Latino Southwest.

> It is important to point out the historical regions and social class pillars of national oppression—the South and Southwest Black and Latino working class. These are the regions with highest concentrations of African American (55%) and Mexican People (50%; and the largest section of the Latino population), where the super-exploitation of Black and Brown labor is the most exploited, least unionized and where political disenfranchisement is the most blatant. Combined, they make up the new and changing face of the U.S. working class in this period of globalization. African American and Latino self-determination in these regions would constitute strong bases of internal opposition against U.S. imperialism.[75]

In New Orleans today, however, contradictions between Blacks and Latinos are exacerbated by the corporate rebuilding plan. In a systematic effort to circumvent Black workers who had already lived in the city, corporations with government contracts import immigrant Latino workers into New Orleans. As the courts are issuing thousands of evictions a day for Black residents, and many cannot re-occupy their apartments or homes in the Lower Ninth Ward and throughout New Orleans, tens of thousands of immigrants are packed three and four each into one hotel room—the new residents of the community. This economic competition orchestrated by the employers is already leading to explosive racial tensions. In several interviews, both a Black worker without a job and a Latino worker packed like a sardine at a boarding house referred to themselves as "slaves." The question is, can the slaves of different races unite?

Gregory Rodriguez recently wrote an article in the *Los Angeles Times* with the provocative title, "La Nueva Orleans: Latino immigrants, many of them here illegally, will rebuild the Gulf Coast—and stay there."[76] Many undocumented Latino workers, brought from Houston to New Orleans, have already been put to work on construction projects and housed in primitive trailer parks with no benefits and no access to government support. They are sometimes low paid, sometimes cheated of their wages, sometimes decently paid, but always a captive labor force under the power and "protection" of white contractors.

In the pre-Katrina turmoil, New Orleans Mayor Ray Nagin, long understood as the candidate of the white downtown business interests, increased the racial tension by telling a group of angry, unemployed Blacks, "How do I make sure that New Orleans is not overrun by Mexican workers?"[77]

His question and answer should have been, "How do I make sure that all the cost-overrun construction projects have their tax money diverted to human needs, and how do we guarantee substantial Black employment and fair treatment of immigrants?"

In sharp contrast to the limited influence of the Black Left, a reactionary, xenophobic, Christian fundamentalist Black bourgeoisie and petty-bourgeoisie with no demands for Black power or self-determination has turned on its own Black poor and working class. They put forth a self-righteous "bootstrapping" ideology that blames Black people for Black poverty and is vociferously anti-Mexican and anti-immigrant, leaving their new buddies in the white power structure unaccountable and whitewashed.

The question is, given the economic desperation many Black people feel, and the power of xenophobia and even "Americanism" in the Black community, will the reactionary or progressive view dominate the debate about Black/Latino relations in New Orleans? Conversely, will progressive forces in the Latino community address frontally the crisis of permanent mass unemployment and incarceration in the Black community and the national policy of hatred of Black workers by most white, corporate employers, who see Blacks as too interested in labor unions, too militant, and not sufficiently "employerized?"

The strategic and programmatic effort to resolve this contradiction among the Black and Latino people will require a two pronged plan—*massive hiring of Black workers in New Orleans, the Gulf Coast, and throughout the United States, and full democratic rights and amnesty for immigrant workers.*

The process of demanding that priority is given to Blacks from Louisiana for new government and construction jobs while also refusing to scapegoat Latino immigrants will require a complex negotiation, reflected in very specific solutions to be worked out on the ground. For example, even before Katrina, Black people in New Orleans had one of the highest unemployment rates in the country, and worked at some of the lowest wages in the country—and now many can't find jobs at all. For many Black people, the key demand is that the government and the private sector create new jobs, since, like their flooded apartments, there are no "old" jobs to return to.

The National Crisis of Anti-Immigrant Hysteria

Throughout 2006, the U.S. Congress has been debating a series of anti-immigrant bills that, as usual, are packaged in the new rhetoric of "reform," which is now code for reaction: as in, "welfare reform" (getting rid of it), "prison reform" (sending more Blacks and Latinos to prison), and "tax reform" (in which the rich pay no taxes).

The election year posturing against Latino immigrants, is taking place at a time of profound changes in the demographics of virtually every urban center in the United States. The accelerated Latino immigration is in part the product of U.S. government action in causing chaos, poverty, and often dictatorship throughout Latin America. Morally, the immigration of Latino immigrants is in fact a return home, a repatriation, a repayment for the entire U.S. history of oppression, enslavement, and confiscation of the lands of Indigenous peoples throughout the west of the United States and the colonization of Central and South America. The national oppression and suffering of Latino and Indigenous peoples in the Americas has been caused by U.S. imperialism—reflected in the "Monroe Doctrine," which the U.S. has used to dominate and exploit Latin countries since 1823, including the theft and annexation of Northern Mexico in 1848.

This policy of racism and Manifest Destiny was continued in the wars of aggression and conquest in Cuba, Puerto Rico, Guatemala, Nicaragua, Guyana, Panama, El Salvador, and virtually every Central and South American nation seeking independence and self-determination. It is extended today through the recent threats to overthrow and assassinate Venezuelan President Hugo Chavez at a time when poverty rates in that country are dramatically reduced and very little emigration out of the country is wanted or needed by its population. Chavez's crime? Challenging the hubris, racism and imperial arrogance of the white settler state to the North.

Both Senate and House immigration bills are reactionary. Their provisions include:

- Creating divisions among undocumented immigrants living in the United States, ranking them in order of "worthiness" based on their length of stay in the U.S.

- Forcing them to register with the Office of Homeland Security, creating in essence 12 million people on probation and parole able to be incarcerated, rounded up, or deported at the whim of the police state.

- Forcing them to pay fines, learn English, and subjugate their native language, and go through a degrading 12 step program to reach the promised land of U.S. citizenship.

Of course the most savvy and principled path for most immigrants will be to avoid the registration process, to continue to live in secrecy, and to have their children, born in the U.S., attain citizenship. The analogies with the runaway slaves should not be lost on the Black community.

National Resistance

The new immigrant rights movement is a powerful, progressive force that must be reckoned with. The Los Angeles Times reported pro-immigrant marches on May 1, 2006 (May Day, International Workers Day) in dozens of cities throughout the U.S. "More than a million immigrants and their supporters did not attend work and participated in the nationwide boycott that disrupted many farms and businesses across the United States. The Times estimated marches and rallies of at least 200,000 to 300,000 in downtown L.A., 300,000 to 400,000 in midtown L.A. that afternoon, 400,000 in Chicago, 20,000 in New York, 50,000 in the Bay Area, 75,000 in Denver, 2500 in Phoenix, 20,000 in Orlando, 10,000 in Miami, 4500 in Atlanta, and 3,000 in New Orleans.[78]

The Latino movement, many of whose members are undocumented immigrants facing enormous threats to their lives and families, came out en masse, with a militant program that included signs that said, "we did not cross the border, the border crossed us," "I demand amnesty, I have done nothing wrong," and placards with pictures of George Bush, Condoleezza Rice, Dick Cheney, and Donald Rumsfeld with the caption, "Wanted for illegally crossing borders."

In Los Angeles, our organization, the Labor/Community Strategy Center, re-issued a strong defense of immigrant rights through our pamphlet, *Immigrant Rights and Wrongs*, (that had been initially written to counter the racist, anti-immigrant Proposition 187 in California in 1994!)[79] As a small contribution to the multitudes of marchers, we were able to mobilize our Drum and Chants Corps and a coalitional marching crew of about 200 people, of whom 50 were Black. But that level of Black participation was an exception. In marches in Los Angeles that we observed, there was very little visible Black participation.

Sabotage of Immigrant Rights by the Two-Party System—and the Urgent Need for Black, and White Allies

Just as the Black movement includes a broad array of political perspectives and class interests, the Latino/Mexican led immigrant rights movement is going through its own internal class and political struggle. How could it be possible that the most impressive national marches of more than a million people could be followed by the most regressive national legislation—in which "border security," "criminalization," "registration," "fines," and "guest worker" programs of indentured servitude are the legislative product of the two-party system? The short answer? *Because there is not a majority or even strong independent Left in the country, and the conservative, racist, white electoral majority that dominates both the Republicans and the Democrats and has sabotaged Katrina Reconstruction is now sabotaging the immigrant rights movement.*

In Los Angeles, for example, the Latino Democratic Party establishment initially opposed the first set of mass marches and opposed the idea of a Latino general strike on May 1. But each time, when the movement took off in spite of their opposition, they marched to the head of the parade to misdirect that movement. Archbishop Roger Mahony opposed the militant general strike march, and organized what was in essence, a watered-down "after work" march on May 1. The "after work" and "non-general strike" marches involved the participation of California Assembly Speaker Fabian Nunez and Los Angeles Mayor, Antonio Villaraigosa. Neither supported the "stop work" demand and the call for amnesty which were put forth by the general strike march that preceded it.

The Democratic Party, with the "Kennedy" wing of the Kennedy McCain bill, has fundamentally agreed with George Bush's plan: registration of immigrants under the Office of Homeland Security, and a "guest worker" program that delivers low-wage labor to U.S. employers but does also offer eventual legalization and citizenship for the "deserving" immigrants.

Where is the discussion of the U.S. seizing of the Mexican border in 1848? Where are the cries of amnesty and full democratic rights that the immigrant rights groups have put forth? They are entirely suppressed from the national congressional and presidential debates. And many immigrant rights groups, in the back pocket of the Democratic Party, condemn "Congress" in general for the sell-out but will not name any Democrats who contributed to that betrayal.

General cries for Black/Latino unity will not suffice. There is a need for Black leadership that is willing to take on the Democrats on Post-Katrina Reconstruction as well as integrating immigrant rights into the centrality of the program of a Third Reconstruction. This would be in the tradition of the late Chicago Mayor Harold Washington who, from 1983 to 1987, initiated one of the first viable Black/Latino progressive coalitions.

In New Orleans, the People's Hurricane Relief Fund is setting a positive example of a South/Southwest, Black/Latino alliance. In the weeks preceding the May 22, 2006 mayoral run-off election between incumbent Ray Nagin and Lt. Governor Mitch Landrieu, PHRF published a programmatic demand document, "Mayoral Campaign Platform for Reconstruction With Justice in New Orleans." Their section "Support the Rights of All Workers and Survivors to Reconstruction Jobs" includes the following demands:

- Establish a program to guarantee full employment at a living wage to all returnees

- Establish hiring preferences for hurricane survivors as they return home, as well as anti-discrimination protections for workers who have responded to the call for reconstruction labor

• End city support for ICE (Immigration Customs Enforcement, formerly the INS) investigations of workplaces and living spaces of reconstruction laborers

• Support safety for laborers and all New Orleanians by ending practices that stop undocumented immigrant workers from calling on emergency and security services; this includes ending collaborations between police and ICE, and making explicit any relationship between the two agencies.

This is a strong, conscious, progressive programmatic formulation and a clear reach-out to Latino workers. This reflects the kind of politics and leadership that the *Black Commentator* and many other progressives and revolutionaries have looked to the Black movement to provide.

Kali Akuno, national outreach coordinator for PHRF, reported that while the New Orleans pro-immigrant march was relatively small by national standards (one press estimate was 3,000 people), PHRF mobilized for it as a priority; and the New Orleans march had a high level of Black participation. As the pro-immigrant marches in the South included 5,000 people in Atlanta and 15-20,000 in Houston (two cities with large numbers of the New Orleans Black diaspora), the opportunity and urgency for the Black/Latino alliance takes center stage. Developing progressive materials that fight for immigrant rights, and turning their people out in the streets to back up their words, the People's Hurricane Relief Fund is providing important leadership on this critical battleground for the future of oppressed nationality unity.

Native American Tribes: Forgotten and Abandoned

Native American tribes that stretch across the Gulf States of Alabama, Louisiana, and Mississippi have become Katrina's forgotten victims.

> "What we are hearing is [that] there has been no contact or minimum contact with most of the tribes," said Robert Holden, of the National Congress of American Indians, who estimates there are several thousand Native Americans living in the hurricane's path...There are at least six federally recognized tribes located in Alabama, Louisiana, and Mississippi. They include the Poarch Band Creek in Alabama, Coshatta Indian Tribe, Jena Band of Choctaw, and Tunicia-Biloxi Tribe in Louisiana, and the Chitimacha Tribe and the Choctaw Indians in Mississippi."[80]

In a tribal area near Chalmette, Louisiana, nine miles east of New Orleans, people were using the local high school as a morgue. While they are in proximity to New Orleans, they didn't hear from anyone for five or six days. There is an urgency to defend the rights of the initial, indigenous inhabitants of North America, who are desperately in need of dedicated allies, new lands adn expanded rights.

Who will reach out to and stand up for the Indigenous peoples? The New Orleans tragedy offers an opportunity to construct a powerful multiracial alliance with leadership from a Black united front that reaches out to immigrants, Mexicans, Hondurans, Salvadoreans, Vietnamese, and Indigenous peoples.[81] This alliance can be strengthened by recruiting antiracist whites who can play a critical role in splitting the "white bloc," to prevent a unified white supremacist backlash. Such an antiracist united front can place the voices of the most oppressed and disenfranchised, and their extraordinary needs and rights, squarely in the face of the system.

11. U.S. Out of Iraq—Bring the War Home!

It is common for progressives to criticize foreign wars for their diversion of funds—such as the fact that the U.S. diverted $71 million from disaster relief funding for New Orleans at the same time as squandering more than $200 billion in the war in Iraq. In a letter written shortly after Katrina struck to Dennis Hastert, the Republican Speaker of the House, Los Angeles Congresswoman Diane Watson was sharply critical of the government's response to Hurricane Katrina. She called for "aggressive federal assistance" and also demanded that the federal government "undertake a thorough reexamination of our nation's homeland security priorities as well as our continuing involvement in Iraq, which continues to be a major drain on the national budget."[82]

But the brutal and unprovoked U.S. invasion of Iraq must be opposed on a more frontal moral and political level than its budgetary costs. The invasion of Iraq is an imperial use of U.S. military and political power in the world. It is built on a foundation of lies: the non-existent weapons of mass destruction; a fraudulent concern about Saddam Hussein's made-in-the-U.S.A. dictatorship when in fact the U.S. sponsors the worst torturers and murderers in the world; and the bold-faced lie that Iraq intended to attack the United States. It is based on the abhorrent concept of preemptive war that ridicules any concept of common international principle. Recent figures indicate more than 2,500 U.S. soldiers have been killed and 14,000 wounded and that 10 percent of all soldiers are seeking psychiatric relief, as working class Black, Latino, Asian/ Pacific Islander, Indigenous, and white kids are sent to kill and be killed in an unjust war. And what of the Iraqi people upon whom this war is being inflicted? Estimates range from 30,000 deaths to as high as 100,000 The invasion of a nation that had no intentions of any aggressive action against the United States, Bush's doctrine of "preemptive war," and the wholesale murder of unarmed, non-combatant civilians are all violations of international law and any minimum standards of human decency. They are war crimes in the classic and legal sense and must be challenged on those terms.

During the height of the Civil Rights Movement, the demand "U.S. Out of Vietnam" was a key civil rights and human rights issue. It was virtually impossible to talk about the racism in U.S. cities without talking about the racism of the war, impossible to decry police brutality at home without challenging U.S. brutality and war crimes in Vietnam. The white antiwar student movement played a critical role in initiating many antiwar marches and helping to build a multiracial antiwar movement. These radical students also played a critical strategic role in turning the elite universities upside down—a serious blow to the system's long-term functioning. But the leadership of Black people—SNCC's "Hell No, We Won't Go!" movement, Muhammad Ali's statement that "No Vietcong Ever Called Me a N——," Martin Luther King's gut-wrenching confession of his own hesitancy to call out U.S.

brutality against the Vietnamese people, and Eartha Kitt's open "insult" of first lady Lady Bird Johnson over the war—brought even greater international isolation and opprobrium upon the United States government, gave encouragement to the Vietnamese people, and gave the Black Liberation Movement tremendous moral authority internationally.

Similarly, the New Orleans crisis cannot be separated from the Iraqi crisis of U.S. brutality. Let's call it what it is: U.S. imperialism is the cause of suffering for oppressed peoples and nations at home and abroad.

Recent CNN polls have reported "fewer than half of Americans believe the U.S. will win the war in Iraq, and 55 percent of those surveyed said it should speed up withdrawal plans and cut spending on the conflict to pay for rebuilding the Gulf Coast after Hurricane Katrina."[83] The moral, political, and economic connections are clear. It would be a major breakthrough in challenging the Bush Administration if all demands for the Black and low-income communities of New Orleans and the Gulf Coast were punctuated by a demand to *immediately withdraw all troops from Iraq and allow the Iraqi people the right of self-determination.*

It is a sad commentary on the state of the Black establishment that a conservative Democrat, John Murtha, has been far more outspoken in his demand for immediate U.S. withdrawal from Iraq, while Reverend Jesse Jackson, ostensibly opposed to the war, has chosen to take a low profile and has done little organizing on the issue. Similarly, Senator Barack Obama has offered a weak and convoluted critique of the initial invasion, followed by his proposal that U.S. troops stay in Iraq to do the invasion right.

> I strongly opposed this war before it began, though many disagreed with me at that time. Today, as Americans grow increasingly impatient with our presence in Iraq, voices I respect are calling for a rapid withdrawal of our troops, regardless of events on the ground.
>
> But I believe that, having waged a war that has unleashed daily carnage and uncertainty in Iraq, we have to manage our exit in a responsible way - with the hope of leaving a stable foundation for the future, but at the very least taking care not to plunge the country into an even deeper and, perhaps, irreparable crisis. I say this not only because we owe it to the Iraqi people, but because the Administration's actions in Iraq have created a self-fulfilling prophecy - a volatile hotbed of terrorism that has already begun to spill over into countries like Jordan, and that could embroil the region, and this country, in even greater international conflict.[84]

And so Bush continues to trap even prominent Black Democrats in his pro-war coalition, so that even Barack Obama who "opposed this war before it began" could not find a way to oppose it once it had started. This is the Bill Clinton "nation building" line on foreign affairs, one now adopted by Obama and Bush. It is tragic to watch the growing internal strife in Iraq, with both Sunni and Shiite Muslims, and Kurds engaged in a brutal internal struggle, fomented by the invasion of the United States. Meanwhile Bush keeps talking about "free elections" to create his hoped-for puppet government as Iraqi society is in a stage of disintegration and civil war, while Democrats Kerry,

Obama, and Hillary Clinton carry out a "cheap-critique-but-basically-agree" tactical plan.*

The movement in New Orleans can strengthen the scope and impact of its demands by incorporating a more systematic and aggressive challenge of the Bush Administration and the Democrats—almost all of whom voted for the war and still oppose withdrawal. A true Third Reconstruction will reflect a Black progressive internationalism—with a strong "U.S. Out of Iraq—Immediate Withdrawal" position. So far, upon reading most of the material from New Orleans and the Gulf Coast, the demand "U.S. Out of Iraq" has not been emphasized, and often is not even mentioned in the demand structure.

It would be a great contribution to the antiwar movement and the movement in New Orleans if the demands for Black survival in the Gulf Coast had a stronger international and human rights focus.

12. The Critical Role of International Allies: Take the Humanitarian Aid from Venezuela and Cuba; Take the Human Rights Case against the United States to the United Nations

The Black community in New Orleans and throughout the Gulf Coast is up against an international alliance of capital,

* Kerry's later, if weak effort, to set a date for a U.S. withdrawal, was an improvement but was soundly rejected by the Democrats, aka the "Party of Opportunism," who asked legitimately, "why didn't you raise this when you ran for the presidency?"

led by the U.S. ruling class. Historically, the search for allies among Blacks, Latinos, Asian/Pacific Islanders, Indigenous peoples, and antiracist whites has been given a major boost by an alliance with progressive forces in the Third World.

The problem, and the political opportunity to move the debate to the left, is that the nations who are most willing and able to help people in New Orleans, and who have made legitimate and impressive offers of aid, are nations hated by the Bush Administration because of their left politics. Thus, the U.S. rejection of concrete offers of help from Cuba and Venezuela expose the bankruptcy of the U.S. social welfare infrastructure and the bipartisan xenophobia that prevents the "great superpower" from admitting any faults or weaknesses of its own. For example, Fidel Castro and the Cuban government offered to send 1,586 Cuban doctors and 36 tons of medical supplies to the victims of Katrina. Predictably, the U.S. government and Bush Administration rejected the offer. Surprisingly, the Congressional Hispanic Caucus responded with a press release on September 8, 2005 titled, "Hispanic Caucus Urges Bush Administration to Accept Cuban Offer of Doctors for Hurricane Relief."[85]

Venezuelan President Hugo Chavez made a similar offer to that of Cuba, stating that "Venezuela could send aid workers with drinking water, food, and fuel to U.S. communities hit by the hurricane." Chavez also offered discount gasoline to "poor Americans suffering from high oil prices and free eye surgery to Americans without access to health care."[86] While clearly in the spirit of international solidarity, this is a very courageous proposal. The United States and CIA think nothing of interfering in the internal affairs of other nations, including floating the "trial balloon" to assassinate Chavez put forth by evangelfascist Pat Robertson. Given the Bush Administration's war on any progressive government in the world and its obsession with socialist Cuba (supported by the reactionary influence of Miami's *gusano* Cuban population) and the "me too" anti-communism of most Democrats, the New Orleans and national movement should openly support the Cuban and Venezuelan governments and peoples and fight the Bush Administration's rejection of their much-needed aid.

Seeking Support from the Third World and the United Nations

During the 1960s, it was international pressure that saved the lives of many civil rights workers. Today, it is international pressure that is a critical strategic component to push the Bush Administration and the Democrats to respect Black demands. Obviously the Bush Administration is the most obstinate about responding to any international demands; but, bogged down and losing in Iraq, isolated in every international body, and losing at the Free Trade Area of the Americas (FTAA) meetings, there are forces inside the U.S. ruling class who are beginning to get it through their thick heads that even the rogue superpower cannot take on the world without profound consequences for U.S. imperialism.

W.E.B. Du Bois, Martin Luther King, Malcolm X, Fannie Lou Hamer, SNCC, and Muhammad Ali, among many others, argued that Black people in the U.S. should ally with the peoples of the Third World. The idea is simple but profound and is based on an empirical and analytical assessment of every presidential election in U.S. history: *inside the United States, even the most powerful alliance of Black, Latino, Asian/Pacific Islander, and Indigenous communities, and a significant number of progressive, antiracist whites, has not been able to forge an electoral majority*. But if we see the entire world as our arena of struggle and organizing, forces inside the United States can build alliances with the revolutionary and progressive peoples and nations of the Third World and progressive forces inside the European Union. This international strategy can construct a worldwide "majority" movement that is capable of countering the enormous military power and ruthlessness of U.S. imperialism and its strong domestic base of support among the majority of whites and significant support in oppressed nationality communities as well.

The United Nations is a central arena for building alliances. Black people in the United States suffer a national and racial oppression so egregious that it cannot be effectively stopped or even mitigated solely through processes that are under the jurisdiction of the United States. They must, as such, as an internally oppressed people, have the right to seek international redress of their grievances.

In 1951, W.E.B. Du Bois, Paul Robeson, and William Patterson, representing the pro-socialist, internationalist tendency in the Black community, were persecuted for their beliefs yet made history in the heart of Cold War reaction with their campaign: "We Charge Genocide: The Historic Petition to the United Nations for Relief from a Crime of the United States Government Against the Negro People."[87] The document charged that the policies of segregation, enforced poverty, mob and police abuse, degradation of culture, and continued subjugation of Black people with the full support of the U.S. government constituted a pattern of human rights abuse. And even though Roy Wilkins, executive director of the NAACP, and others in the Black establishment fused their anti-communism and patriotism by red-baiting Du Bois, Robeson, and Patterson, they could not prevent the charges from influencing world opinion and helping set the stage for later civil rights victories, as well as ongoing scrutiny of the U.S. for human rights violations.

In the 1960s, Malcolm X also advocated the view that Black people are an oppressed nation with the right to land and self-determination. He rejected a restrictive theory of civil rights under the U.S. constitution as the master narrative for Black liberation. While he supported specific legal reforms under the mantle of civil rights, he felt the theoretical and analytical rubric was too limiting and ultimately self-defeating because of its dependence on the U.S. courts, capitalism, and the white majority. Instead, he advocated approaching the United Nations, and calling on the international community in general, and Third World nations in particular, to require the U.S. to stop its racist policies towards Blacks in the U.S., or suffer sanctions. Today, there are voices in New Orleans and throughout the Black community who are urging dispersed evacuees to see themselves as part of a Black Diaspora movement that is seeking international support, and, if necessary, calling for U.N. sanctions against the U.S. for human rights violations and criminal negligence against a nationally and racially constituted minority.

Saladin Muhammad of Black Workers for Justice argues that since the United States decided to reallocate massive resources for an unjust war in Iraq, de-funded FEMA, and refused $250 million to the Army Corps of Engineers to improve the New Orleans levees, it, in essence, "decided" to let Black people in New Orleans die.

> U.S. imperialism has thus decided that it has the sole right to decide if the majority of African American and working class people and communities in the Gulf Coast Region have the human and political right to survive or not. This is clearly an international human rights question where the demand for self-determination must be applied as part of the resolution...asking the United Nations to conduct an investigation into the circumstances of the Katrina disaster to determine if the U.S. is guilty of human rights violations.[88]

One tactical possibility would be to make an immediate alliance with the Alliance of Small Island States that is demanding that the United Nations take the most urgent actions on global warming and provide international relief to address the massive flooding of entire nations and peoples caused by the fossil fuel emissions of the advanced capitalist countries, especially the United States. Another tactic would be to support Venezuelan president Hugo Chavez's serious proposal that the United Nations be moved out of the United States to a Third World site to set the conditions for a greater world democracy and to mitigate the intimidating presence of the imperial bully. As with all major, radical, structural, and counterhegemonic demands raised by the Left, and the Black Left at this point in history, the short-term possibilities of winning the actual reform, the actual change in policy, are very remote given the formidable balance of forces lined up against us. But agitational demands that are raised with all seriousness, accompanied by a concrete organizing plan, and used to win real people to a movement, are essential building blocks that can allow us to climb out of this abyss, one step at a time.

This greater emphasis on the role of the United Nations should not underestimate the domination of that body by the U.S., especially in the Security Council. The present Bush-appointed U.S. ambassador to the United Nations, John Bolton, is determined to destroy the organization itself. But we have seen in the unprecedented U.N. opposition to U.S. threats to invade Iraq, and the worldwide condemnation of the U.S. invasion and its pathetic "coalition of the willing," that U.S. hegemony is on the decline. The U.N., with its limits and contradictions, is rising in importance as an arena in which to challenge U.S. imperialism at home and abroad.

Conclusion: Movement Building and Counterhegemonic Demand Development

Snapshots as We Approach the First Anniversary of the Katrina Catastrophe

The situation on the ground in New Orleans is always in flux. Society and history move through the struggle of opposites. Here are some last observations, the opening chapters in a never ending story.

The Whitewashing of Black Oppression in New Orleans by the Democrats, Labor, and Some on the Left: The Primary Obstacle to Progress

As grassroots groups in New Orleans and the Gulf Coast struggle to be heard, the capitulation of liberal and moderate

Democrats to a corporatist rebuilding process, and the confidence and arrogance of the right-wing Republicans and Democrats is exacerbating the ongoing crisis on the ground. The suppression of an antiracist analysis is part of an ideological offensive by Democratic Party liberals, and even some groups on the Left, that constitute an ideological offensive against a Black Reconstruction or any form of a Black political ascension and fight back.

An October *New York Times* article, "Liberal Hopes Ebb in Post-Storm Debate on Poverty," by Jason DeParle, described liberal capitulation in painful detail:

> As Hurricane Katrina put the issue of poverty onto the national agenda, many liberal advocates wondered whether the floods offered a glimmer of opportunity. The issues they most cared about—health care, housing, jobs, and race—were suddenly staples of the news, with President Bush pledged to "bold action."
>
> But what looked like a chance to talk up new programs is fast becoming a scramble to save the old ones. Conservatives have already used the storm for causes of their own, like suspending requirements that federal contractors have affirmative action plans and pay locally prevailing wages. And with federal costs for rebuilding the Gulf Coast estimated at $200 billion, Congressional Republican leaders are pushing for spending cuts, with programs like Medicaid and food stamps especially vulnerable.[89]

During the First and Second Reconstructions, the fight for Black liberation was tied, inexorably, to a fight against white supremacy as national policy. It was rarely an attack on "white people" in general, even though the majority of white folks were both the beneficiaries and agents of white supremacy. Certainly the tendency for Black people to generalize, to place the blame on "the system," "the white man," "the white power structure" and also "white folks" was based on a telling critique of the vast majority of whites' active participation in racist institutions and the endemic racism of white culture and white society as a whole. Black people, both as individuals and as a people, have spent many centuries navigating the complexities of white society as a matter of life and death. When combined with the inordinate generosity of Black culture, this has led to a nuanced assessment of white people and their behaviors. If Black folks came to fear and hate the Klan, they also came to know that the white Radical Republicans were dependable and passionate allies, antiracist whites were essential participants in the underground railroad under Black leadership, many white generals and military officers helped to free the slaves and gave their lives in that pursuit, and John Brown's body was sacrificed to arm and free the Black slaves. Any white organizers who have been given the gift of being a part of the Second Reconstruction, the Civil Rights and the Black Liberation Movement, can attest to the generosity and courage of the Black masses and their unquestioned ability to distinguish between white friend and foe.

But rarely is such generosity reciprocated by white liberals, white labor, and even some in the multi-racial Left who believe that "class unity" is best served by posing a color blind, metaphysically "unified" working class or movement, in which, according to this view, too much talk about race, especially the oppressed Black race, is harmful to the greater, if never clearly defined, broader goal.

As such, perhaps the greatest blow to the movement is put forth by those who try to deny the obvious—that Hurricane Katrina has been one of the great blows to the Black community in the 21st century, that New Orleans was a majority Black city and a hub of Black southern and national culture, and that the Right of Return means the right of the Black New Orleans Diaspora to return to their own Black city. Those simple and undeniable truths are now being whited out by a hostile white majority in the country, an ascendant white minority with hopes of becoming the new majority in New Orleans, and perhaps most disturbingly, by some in the labor movement and the Left.

At a time when an Afrocentric discourse is so needed as a simple baseline of political logic in the Katrina conversation, there has been an intellectual evasion by members of the media, liberal organizations, organized labor, and even some Black Democratic Party forces who have made a conscious choice to transform all references into a neutral toned picture of "the survivors," "the poor," "the working class" and "the dispersed." *This whitewashing of Black liberation is the primary ideological obstacle to any positive resolution of the problem.*

One example among many, among thousands, is the clear statement on a "color blind" view of the problem put forth by a prominent New Orleans labor official—in which the conscious denial of a Black reality was articulated with such force and clarity.

On Saturday, October 29, 2005, Pacifica Radio broadcast a statewide show on organized labor, and forthcoming ballot initiatives in California—a collaboration between KPFK in Los Angeles and KPFA in Northern California. Louis Reine, the secretary-treasurer of the Louisiana AFL-CIO, was one of the guests. Reine described a march and rally that took place in New Orleans that day led by the AFL-CIO, the NAACP, and the Reverend Jesse Jackson. Reine discussed the need for union jobs, called for the re-institution of the Davis-Bacon prevailing wage standards, and made the case for more federal aid to rebuild New Orleans. In his remarks, he did not discuss the problems of New Orleans from an antiracist perspective, nor mention the specific needs and demands of the vast majority of the oppressed, the Black residents of New Orleans. As a co-host of the program, I pressed him on that omission. The quotes below are from the transcripts of that radio broadcast.

> *Eric Mann*: Hi, this is Eric Mann in Southern California. How are you doing? My question to you is that given that 84 percent of the poorest people in New Orleans were Black, how much of the rally focused on the racism of the system, and how much of it even called the Democrats as well as the Republicans into accountability for not taking a stand on, you know, that the Right of Return is primarily the right of Black people to return to New Orleans? Was that emphasized in the march?
>
> *Louis Reine*: No. Our call is that all people should be treated fairly. A lot of what we saw happen in New Orleans in the first days after Katrina and the levee broke was as much about economics as they were color. It was about poor people who didn't have a means of transportation. Nobody had a plan to allow for them to evacuate in an event like this.

> And hurricanes, natural disasters, they don't know color, they don't know economic standards. And everybody who has suffered through this needs help. It's not whether you're Black or you're white, or you're male or you're female, this, the greatest country in the world, should step up and give a helping hand to its citizens when they suffer a disaster. Whether that's a hurricane and a flood in Louisiana, or an earthquake in California, or a flood in the Middle East. When citizens of the United States go through a disaster, it's the time that all people need to come together, stand together, and help our neighbors and our friends.[90]

The statement by an official of the Louisiana AFL-CIO that "hurricanes, natural disasters, they don't know color, they don't know economic standards" reflects a prevalent view in the movement that feels it is best to reject ("liquidate") the structural demands of Blacks as an oppressed people. It stems from a strategic view that the best way to "unite" a multi-racial working class and a multi-national country is to find issues with a "common denominator." According to this view, structural demands that prioritize the super-exploitation and super-oppression of Black people in the U.S., demands for Reparations, land, self-determination, priority in hiring and aggressive affirmative action are seen as "divisive." Instead, it is argued that it is best to reach out to "everybody" in a way that, consciously or not, prioritizes an appeal to whites, even reactionary whites. The liquidation of special, structural Black demands does nothing to organize white workers in a truly progressive direction, or to raise their antiracist consciousness. Instead, it encourages white supremacy and contributes to a sense of isolation and abandonment in Black communities.

Dr. Robert Bullard of Clark Atlanta University supports the Afrocentric view in opposition to the "colorblind," "all-class" perspective. In surveying the all-Black scene in the Superdome, where Black people were piled upon Black people, he observed,

> Now, how is it that New Orleans is 70% Black and 30% white but the Superdome was all Black? Where were all the white folks if this is supposed to be about 'the poor'? Of course, class is a factor, but in the United States, race trumps class if you want to understand how the system operates.[91]

Curtis Muhammad of Community Labor United expressed a similar view. At a public event in Los Angeles he told the audience, "Let's be clear. The victims of Katrina were the poorest of the poor and the blackest of the Black."[92]

At a time when many white and even some Black elected officials are choosing to avoid a discussion of the "ethnic cleansing" of New Orleans, as many Black activists call it, it is the Right that is not intimidated about talking about race, or putting forth racist observations. Housing and Urban Development Secretary Alphonso Jackson clearly acknowledged, "Whether we like it or not, New Orleans is not going to be 500,000 people for a long time...New Orleans is not going to be as Black as it was for a long time, if ever again."[93] What seems like an objective observation by a high ranking Bush Administration official is of course a tip-off of national policy, a decision that New Orleans will never be as Black as it once was if the federal government has anything to say about it.

Ironically, throughout U.S. history, we have seen that during Black-led progressive periods—such as the First and Second Reconstructions—many white workers have been won over to a broader left program based on a profound understanding of Black liberation and white supremacy, and they have fought for Black demands as part of an overall revolutionary, and at times, socialist strategy. In both the First and Second Reconstructions, the major gains for Blacks also led to substantial gains for the white poor and working class. Conversely, we have seen time and time again that when people in "the movement" or forces inside the AFL-CIO and Democratic Party have told Black people to drop their specific, structural, and revolutionary demands in "the interests of unity," that has contributed to the weakening of the Black movement, and the overall U.S. Left. Meanwhile, the whites, especially the white working and middle classes, left to their own racial devices, move further towards white supremacy and the embrace of the Right.

Any "labor" or allegedly progressive perspective that claims that hurricanes don't discriminate against "rich or poor," that adamantly refuses to challenge white supremacy and the Democrats, that talks about "citizens" at a time when so many of the oppressed and its leaders are undocumented immigrants, and that gratuitously interjects that "this is the greatest country in the world" at a time when the U.S. is increasingly reactionary and isolated in the world does a grave disservice to the movement in New Orleans, and to the Black Nation under attack.

Will Anyone Challenge the Democrats?

In the electoral arena, a more hopeful, if still remote, tactical option would be a Black-led, independent, progressive presidential candidacy. Harry Belafonte, at the Congressional Black Caucus and in forums in New York since Katrina, has raised the idea of an independent, Black-led progressive political party to run a presidential candidate in the 2008 elections.

At the 35th Annual Legislative Conference meeting of the Congressional Black Caucus in Washington, D.C., September 21-24, 2005, Belafonte explained to an all-Democratic meeting, and in front of U.S. Senator Hillary Clinton (D-N.Y.), his deep concerns about how the Democrats have sold out the Black voters and his call for a "second party," in that the two major parties function as one.

> The wreckage that is taking place down in the Gulf region is not the only wreckage that exists. Perhaps the most distracting, most important wreckage to look at, to me, is the wreckage of the Democratic Party.
>
> I've been a Democrat all my life. I have no faith in the Republicans. But the Democratic Party has not always been our friend. As a matter of fact, a lot of what we had to struggle against is the possession of power of Democrats who came from the South. When we showed them the tenaciousness and conviction and the sense of big purpose this nation had to go through to transform our conditions, all those Democrats ran off and became Republicans. That punishment for what we were trying to achieve as a people continues to play itself out.
>
> Of course as Dr. King says we're integrating into a burning house, so what do we want to do about it? He said

> we're going to have to go out and become the firemen. Well, maybe that's what our humble task is—to find the truck, get the hose, and know where to turn it on. I'm not that interested in [the Congressional elections of] 2006. It's just another date for a lot of rich folks and for a lot of opportunists to go out and do their thing yet again. I'm interested in something much bigger. I think we have to serve notice that we're looking for a second party.[94]

The specifics of a challenge to the Democrats in the presidential elections will require a complex strategic and tactical discussion. In 2004 I wrote *The 2004 Elections: A Challenge to the U.S. Left* in which I argued for the Left to actively support John Kerry, "without illusions," as part of a broad united front against the arch-Right led by George W. Bush.[95] I stand by that assessment, based on the particular time, place, and conditions, despite Kerry's raising opportunism to a principle, developments I had fully anticipated, and which did not change the broader united front urgency of trying to vote out a neo-fascist clique. I also argued that the narrow white populism of Ralph Nader and the absence of any real mechanisms to build a people of color led, effective independent party, did not offer a viable third choice. If in 2008 there is an Al Gore/John McCain race, the choices for the Left will again be complex, but a possible united front with the Democrats again will be at least worth considering. But what if it is a Hillary Clinton/McCain race? Many progressives are already declaring their commitment to work against Clinton in the primaries, to launch an anti-war candidate against her, and if she is elected, to refuse to lend her candidacy support because of her rank opportunism and support for the war in Iraq (hardly unique qualities among today's Democrats). But in all the calculations and hypotheticals, our hopes are greatly restricted by the profound weakness of the U.S. Left, the great limits of the electoral system for building popular power, and the remote possibility of an independent Black-led presidential campaign.

If, in fact, Harry Belafonte, one of the great Left-wing thinkers and advocates of our generation (whose brilliance spans his early comradeships with Paul Robeson and W.E.B. Du Bois) or actor/activist Danny Glover, or Georgia Congressperson Cynthia McKinney announced a serious run for the presidency then that would mark a major turning point in U.S. history and would warrant the enthusiastic support of a multiracial Left. It could be the first serious answer to the racist, states' rights interventions of Strom Thurmond in 1948 and George Wallace in 1968, who no longer need to initiate a third party challenge because their views are so well reflected in the Republican Party and the Democratic Leadership Council. A Belafonte or Glover or McKinney candidacy, or even better, a combination of them for president and vice president, could attract millions of people (currently trapped inside the sterile two-party debate) and place the whole system on trial. It would not be without risks, for the punishing of the Democrats for decades if not centuries of sabotage, while attractive and justified, must be thought through in the realm of strategy and tactics as well. Still, another four years of the Republican Right, which was not averted by the efforts to elect Kerry, or another four years of Democratic opportunism and collaboration with the right-wing agenda, would be worth risking if the Third

Party (or as Belafonte chooses to call it, a "Second party") insurgency could really get off the ground. That would require a significant level of funding and organizational professionalism, and would encourage grassroots social movements in the cities and rural areas. Such an insurgency could re-energize the moral authority of the Black community and the progressive/Left in the U.S.

Our dilemma is not how to cross that bridge, but the small probability of having that opportunity. Belafonte's challenge is still many steps away from a viable national campaign and he has, as of yet, given no indications that his serving notice on the Democrats would include his own bid for the presidency. Still, Belafonte's challenge, to both the Congressional Black Caucus and Hillary Clinton, is of historical significance. It has been one of the few frontal challenges to the Democrats by a prominent Black progressive and Leftist, and offers a model of electoral insurgency which must be seriously considered as part of a future tactical arsenal as we struggle to move forward.

The Right of Return One More Time—Can We Reverse the Whitewashing of New Orleans?

The catastrophic reality loses none of its urgency through the necessity of its repetition—a major human-made disaster has allowed the United States government, as a matter of national policy, to facilitate, and refuse to reverse the forced removal of some 250,000 former Black residents of New Orleans—who are now scattered throughout the U.S. as a Black New Orleanian Diaspora. The Right of Return of the

Black masses to New Orleans is the central challenge facing the Black movement and its allies today.

As Black community activists understood within a few days after Katrina hit, New Orleans is in the process of a massive, reactionary demographic shift. As the Washington Post reports, the city is becoming "richer and whiter." As we approach the first anniversary of Katrina, the total population of New Orleans itself is estimated by some to be as few as 150,000 on-the-ground residents, most likely no more than 200,000—at the lowest, only 33 percent of its former population, and at the most, no more than 50 percent. Again, just that level of difficulty of ascertaining accurate demographic data from key New Orleans activists, journalists, and attorneys reflects a city, and a broader society, in flux and chaos. Three demographic trends break down as follows:

1) Declining Black population. Some grassroots "ballpark" estimates indicate that the Black population may have fallen as low as 50 percent, and some fear it may be even lower when more accurate statistics are available. So, by all estimates, the city's Black population has declined from almost 70% to no more than a slight majority and perhaps even less than half of the total population. If the city was once 500,000 people, and was 67 percent Black, the initial Black population was approximately 350,000. If the city is now no more than 200,000 people and is no more than 50 percent Black, that means that the present Black population is no more than 100,000. By simple and tragic subtraction, that means as many as 250,000 Black people are missing, dispersed, and desperately trying to return.

2) Rising white population as a percentage of the whole. After Katrina, besides the majority Black districts that were destroyed and the greater number of white homes and neighborhoods that remained standing and viable, many of the more affluent whites were able to evacuate their families very close to New Orleans, often to its suburbs. Many have been able to commute back into the city—to jobs they have retained! Many are discussing re-buying in New Orleans, as well as keeping their second homes outside of the city. While the total of whites is also less than before, as a percentage of the whole it is estimated that the city has gone from 30 percent white to as high as 50 percent white.

3) The dynamics of white privilege and Black national oppression. Many poor whites were devastated by Katrina. They do not have the privileges to function as a coherent collective body and need to tie their hopes to the Black lead fight to rebuild the city. Many more affluent white residents who lost their homes were able to move in with other white, suburban families, either friends or relatives. They used their cell phones to call their insurance agents, and again for many, were able to get rapid settlements of their claims and use the money to reinvest in their future. For most Black, low-income residents, the majority of them have been dispersed to Baton Rouge, Shreveport, Houston, and Atlanta. They do not have the connections, the sense of race and class privilege, and the facility with the system's institutions and rules to get back on their feet. Many could not afford home insurance. Many were renters. Even if they finally get an insurance settlement, it barely covers their mortgage. They are left with little or no surplus and no ability to buy their way back into New Orleans.

Almost a year after Katrina, the Lower Ninth Ward and many other areas of New Orleans that were predominantly Black are still abandoned, with their former residents desperately trying to bring them back to life.

> For much of the Lower Ninth Ward, the block is empty and silent, with no electricity, no drinkable water, no gas, no FEMA trailers, and no signs of rebuilding on a street where many families owned their homes for generations. By contrast, white residents of nearby Lakeview, with their FEMA trailers and government benefits have told the press, 'I think this country has done a wonderful job providing for us.'"[96]

The 1965 Voting Rights Act is Being Violated En Masse

At a press conference, shortly before the May 20, 2006 Mayoral Run-off election, Muriel Lewis of the National Association of Katrina Evacuees, Damon Hewitt of the NAACP Legal Defense and Educational Fund, and Ron Walters, Director of the African American Leadership Institute, documented massive and persistent voting rights abuses in the April 22, 2006 primary election for mayor and other offices in New Orleans. Ron Walters explained, "Thousands of ballots were invalidated in this election system, approved by the Justice Department, because of either voter ID problems or the late receipt of absentee ballots."

Many Black residents from out of the city took buses back to New Orleans to vote. Still, Black voting was only 31 percent of all those registered, whereas white voters had 48 percent to 50 percent turnout.

Given the fact that prior to Katrina 84 percent of New Orleans poor had been Black, and that Blacks have been by far the most dispersed community following Katrina, the Black vote was remarkable. It reflected the resiliency of the Black voters who came in buses to register and vote, many of whom could have used absentee satellite voting but wanted to make sure that their vote was counted. Civil rights attorneys brought suit in federal court to stop the elections. The federal courts rejected those motions. Reverend Jesse Jackson campaigned to hold off the elections until more Black voters could return. His proposal was rejected.

But the fundamental question remains: should the election have been allowed to take place with so many Black residents dispersed throughout the U.S., with so little federal effort to rebuild their communities or bring them back to the city, and with so many election violations to prevent the absentee voters from having their votes counted? And what will be the future federal remedies as the federal Voting Rights Act of 1965 is up for reauthorization before Congress in 2006, before it expires in 2007. Key provisions include pre-clearance before any state can change voting regulations, subject to federal review and bilingual language assistance to voters in communities where there is a concentration of eligible voters who are not "English proficient." Given that so many Black former prisoners have been denied the vote, that the federal courts did not overturn the New Orleans elections or Bush's theft of votes in Florida, and that an "English only" backlash against immigrants is very possible, a national coalition to prioritize the expansion of voting rights, and the prevention of crippling amendments is an urgent priority.

The Re-election of Ray Nagin as Mayor of New Orleans

For movement organizers in New Orleans, the run-off election for mayor, between incumbent Ray Nagin and Lieutenant Governor Mitch Landrieu was filled with ambivalence, contradictions, and a hoped for better alternative. On the one hand, Nagin had been distrusted in the Black community, not just because he received 80 percent of the white vote in the previous mayoral election, but because he was seen as the candidate of the privileged and the business elite. While during the immediate catastrophe of the Hurricane he had made some militant, if temporary, representations on behalf of the Black community towards the Bush Administration, and after the mass dispersal, talked about bringing New Orleans back as a "chocolate city" he even backtracked and said his view of "chocolate" was a Black base with white milk—and the beat went on from there. His anti-Latino remarks and his refusal to come up with a clear commitment to rebuild the Black sections of the city created grave distrust among progressive activists and organizers of all races.

Mitch Landrieu is a moderate liberal in the Kennedy mold, the Lieutenant Governor of the state, and part of a powerful political family that includes his sister, Mary Landrieu, who is the United States Senator from Louisiana, and his father, Moon Landrieu who was the last white mayor of New Orleans. One line against him was "we don't want one family to dominate the politics of the city and state." Landrieu, who had a decent record on civil rights, reached out to Black voters. Conversely, at first, the support for Nagin was at best lukewarm among Black voters, and some actively campaigned for Landrieu.

Bishop Paul Morton of Greater St. Styphen Full Gospel Baptist Church, and more than a dozen other clergy, held a press conference and issued a statement addressing the racial dynamics of the election.

> We realize that African Americans will question why we are supporting a white candidate over a black candidate... We would like to support an African-American candidate whom we thought would welcome everyone home and support the development of all of our neighborhoods. We would like to support an African-American candidate who can help us rebuild our homes, hospitals and schools. But we can't find one.[97]

On the other hand, given the massive displacement of Black voters, and the material force of racial symbolism, many Black organizers felt that the election of a white liberal to replace Nagin would send the wrong signal to the Black community, and would leave the Bush Administration with a clever observation that the Black community in New Orleans blamed Nagin for the disaster. Many antiracist organizers of all nationalities indicated they would have been open to, if not enthused about, a Landrieu candidacy if he had in fact gone out of his way to court the Black vote by making a firm and clear commitment to rebuild the Lower Ninth Ward and other Black majority parishes. But Landrieu refused, and he and Nagin ran a classic, if cordial, campaign of evasion—each claiming that they agreed on all the issues, thus, the only question was who was best able to lead New Orleans into its rebuilding phase.

In the end, Nagin won a close race, garnering 59,460 votes (52 percent) to Landrieu's 54,130 votes (48 percent.) It was estimated that Nagin won with 80 percent of the Black vote and 20 percent of the white vote, with Landrieu's the mirror opposite—with 80 percent of the white vote and 20 percent of the Black vote, indicating that even with the massive dislocations, the Black electorate is still a force to be reckoned with. During the election, many from the People's Hurricane Relief Fund acknowledged that their campaign platform to impact the Mayoral elections was not very successful as each candidate refused to appear at a candidate's night to even debate such a clear programmatic alternative. In the fight to rebuild New Orleans, the job for the movement will be to build a strong united front from below in which both Nagin and Landrieu will be pressured to become key allies, if only tactical ones.

Since the election, Black New Orleans' worst fears have been realized—Nagin has been literally missing in action. But to the degree he has surfaced, he has supported a downtown business elite plan for a far smaller, whiter, more affluent and business-friendly New Orleans. Black evacuees are now faced with more systematic and brutal police opposition to their return to the city.

The Crisis in Summary

The situation in New Orleans makes hyperbole impossible. Hurricane watchers say this is the worst natural disaster in U.S. history. Geologists, global warming scientists, and experts on levee construction argue that the city will be hit with future Category 4 and 5 storms, and even the rebuilt levees are structurally unsound. The U.S. passion for fossil fuel consumption that will require a literal cutting in half of all greenhouse gases today continues unabated at the governmental and mass consumption levels. Congressman John Conyers says that failure of the U.S. to respond to an abandoned and endangered Black community is one of the worst civil rights violations in U.S. history. The complete failure of the Bush administration and FEMA combines the incompetence, maliciousness, and racism of a declining empire. While New Orleans has played a critical role in Black national development and has been called by its Black residents the most Afrocentric city in the U.S., it is also a jewel of the U.S. ruling class, with its commercialized mass culture trying to paper over its indigenous roots, its gambling casinos and its Mardi Gras transformed into a symbol of the party-until-we-die motif, as the New Orleans ports are more important to the system than the New Orleans population.

An urgent June 1, 2006 media release from the Katrina Information Network (KIN), explains the urgency of the situation in its title alone: "More Hurricanes Coming: As Services Decrease Katrina's Displaced form Survivor's Councils and Get Organized."

> With the coming of the 2006 hurricane season, internally displaced survivors of last year's storms are struggling to maintain their basic needs. Thousands of families who have been living in government subsidized apartments face eviction due to changes in FEMA's housing requirements. Over 50,000 families were scheduled to be evicted starting Thursday June 1st, the official start of the 2006 hurricane season. Meanwhile, many continue to struggle in the harsh conditions of trailer parks, far from decent jobs and threatened by future storms and budget cuts. Lack of transportation, the closure of public housing and a difficult job market have all compounded the trauma of last year's storms. Even emergency services such as health care and counseling are becoming harder to find... Access to government subsidized housing within New Orleans has become a major point of contention between residents who need affordable housing and HUD officials who have refused to re-open housing facilities.
>
> Organizations of hurricane evacuees are now faced with the problem that many services available right after Katrina are no longer being offered. "Because its not called an emergency right now people are no longer volunteering to send supplies down. We have had to work even harder to get the supplies we need to these communities" stated Muriel Lewis, director of NAKE. Although the Survivor's Council model is growing in number and providing a much-needed venue for people to advocate for themselves, these community groups remain largely without funding or national support.[98]

What kind of country, government, political system can allow a city of almost 500,000 people to shrink by half before our very eyes, and do virtually nothing to even try to recreate it; to allow more than 250,000 Black people from the African Diaspora to become part of the New Orleans Diaspora and do virtually nothing to assert, let alone implement, an effective Right of Return?

So Where is the Hope? Grassroots Initiatives, Coalitional Formations, Programmatic Demands, and a Long-Term Political Perspective

Grassroots Initiatives

Tens of thousands of Black people get in buses and come back to New Orleans where they can barely afford an overnight hotel room. They stay with their friends or family in the city, try to return to their destroyed homes and still demand the right to vote—a right it took them 246 years to win and another 100 to even have a chance to implement. The resiliency and courage of the Black people in the U.S., an oppressed people inside a white settler state, is the stuff of which legends and history are made.

Groups like the Common Ground Collective and the work of Mama D in the Treme district reflect efforts to rebuild, home by home, block by block. Hundreds of volunteers are still coming to New Orleans to help out, building hope with their bare hands. As just a small example, Mark Anthony Johnson and Francisca Porchas from the Strategy Center went to New Orleans for a week during the 2005 Thanksgiving break, to work with community residents to scrub off mold, pick up garbage and refuse, and help individual homeowners who were trying to make something positive out of the wreckage. They returned overwhelmed by the courage of the community. Mark Anthony returned for another week and a group of us plan to return to New Orleans for the first anniversary of Katrina. These small efforts are part of a far larger effort in which hundreds of young people from throughout the country, many of whom have stayed for far longer times, have been giving hands-on help while still others have moved to the city to become permanent participants in the reconstruction efforts.

The Katrina Information Network reports, "under these harsh conditions, thousands of people throughout the Gulf States are organizing themselves into 'Survivor's Councils' and working to solve the problem of their communities."[99] Civil rights legal teams have been building significant legal challenges to the collapse of federal aid to Katrina survivors. They have set up Voter Empowerment Centers in Baton Rouge, Atlanta, and Houston, and are in touch with tens of thousands of dispersed voters and former residents who want to continue to exercise their rights. People are coming forth to stop the evictions and FEMA's unlawful and immoral curtailment of the one year rule that guarantees paid housing and protection from evictions. Again, it is the masses who are fighting for their rights on every front, and providing the initiative and plaintiffs for all the legal challenges.

Lawyers for New Orleans evacuees have filed suit in Houston, asking a federal court to stop FEMA from ending housing benefits for tens of thousands of people who fled the flooding of Hurricane Katrina. The evacuees had been issued 12-month housing vouchers by local governments but are now being told by FEMA they must pay rent or leave. The suit, brought by Cadell and Chapman, a private law firm, and a consortium of public interest legal groups points out that in the past FEMA has issued housing benefits for longer than a year. The immediacy of this government "free market" demand—"pay up or leave"—has galvanized some

New Orleans evacuees and has the potential to generate a more comprehensive movement. But even then, the movement must address what happens if they "win" the lawsuit and the federal government agrees to extend the housing vouchers for the full year. What will happen then, since there are no plans underway to even begin to rebuild most of the Black sections of New Orleans, and the evacuees cannot survive well in their new surroundings either?

Kali Akuno of PHRF and the Malcolm X Grassroots Movement observed that while the New Orleans population may be about half Black and half white during the week, on the weekends tens of thousands of Black New Orleanians return to the city from Baton Rouge, Shreveport, Houston, and Atlanta, to hang around in their old neighborhoods, to relocate and rebuild old residences, help others fight evictions, and just retain their social and physical ties to their long-standing home. The tens of thousands of dispersed voters who came back to the city to exercise their right to vote again reflect the great spontaneous energy of a dispersed community desperately in need of greater organizational leadership and private and public resources. For at least tens of thousands of the New Orleans Black Diaspora, the struggle is far from over.

Organizations: The Key to Mobilizing Grassroots Power and Placing the Most Structural Demands on the System

Katrina's Legacy cannot possibly catalogue and list, let alone analyze the specific organizations on the ground in New Orleans and the Gulf Coast, to assess their roles and contributions, nor is it within its objectives. Still, having been in touch with many on-the-ground organizers in New Orleans and the Gulf Coast, and having our own members attend many of the key meetings from the Congressional Black Caucus to regional meetings in South Carolina to several trips to the city itself, a partial listing of groups on the ground is given to indicate the scope of the work.

There is an extensive network of groups on the ground working in a broad united front to continue to press demands against the system in New Orleans and the Gulf Coast. These groups include People's Hurricane Relief Fund and Oversight Coalition, Families and Friends of Louisiana's Incarcerated Children, Common Ground Collective, and the Katrina Information Network. The movement also includes ACLU, ACORN, African American Leadership Project, American Friends Service Committee, Black Activist Coalition on Katrina, Black Workers for Justice, Citizens for a Strong New Orleans East, Critical Resistance, Deep South Center for Environmental Justice, Environmental Advocates for Human Rights, Incite! Women of Color Against Violence, Louisiana Environmental Action Network, Malcolm X Grassroots Movement, Mama D's work in the Treme community, Mississippi Workers' Center for Human Rights, NAACP, NAACP Legal Defense and Educational Fund, National Association of Katrina Evacuees, National Lawyer's Guild, New Orleans Network, NO-HEAT New Orleans Housing Emergency Action Team, Orleans Parish Prison Reform Coalition, People's Institute for Survival and Beyond, People's Organizing Committee, Project South, Southern Echo, Safe Streets/Strong Communities, Saving

Ourselves (SOS), Solidarity, The Advancement Project, US Human Rights Network, and several informal networks of Black churches. The future is in these group's hands.

The Evolution of a Grassroots Program

Katrina's Legacy, from its earliest version in September 2005 (as *Letter in Support of a Black Reconstruction in New Orleans and the Gulf Coast*), has placed its primary emphasis on demand development, and to encourage the broadest possible movement discussion about political program—which is the concrete reflection of one's analysis, strategy, and tactics. Vibrant social movements are built around creative and militant demands placed on the system. Key demands give a social movement a sense of orientation, to answer the most commonly asked question: "What is it that you people want?"

The Right of Return has shaped the demands of the People's Hurricane Relief Fund since the first days of Katrina, and demands for rent subsidies, income supports, massive social programs, and community oversight of the rebuilding and reconstruction project have been on the table—and rejected by the system—from the jump. But as the movement has evolved, PHRF has worked to evolve its programmatic focus, demands that can hopefully coalesce a broader progressive, antiracist movement in the city. In April 2006, PHRF issued a new programmatic document: "Mayoral Campaign Platform for Reconstruction with Justice in New Orleans." It asked both mayoral candidates, Nagin and Landrieu, to campaign on "concrete elements of the

Right of Return. Without a commitment to these actions, candidate's claims about 'bringing New Orleanians home' are meaningless."

It was a reflection of the balance of power between the social movements and the elected officials that this program did not achieve its immediate objectives—in that neither candidate felt compelled to address the many specific demands of the Platform. But if it serves to help unify a movement or even a tendency in the movement, it can have great impact in the future.

The program, which is available in greater detail from PHRF, is organized into broad demand categories.

- Reopen and recreate housing in New Orleans

- Reunite New Orleans families

- Justice and safety for Katrina survivors (convene a commission to address issues of racial inequality in New Orleans and the state of Louisiana)

- Community-based democratic process for all reconstruction decisions (acknowledge the injustice of these elections, demand satellite voting for all elections affecting New Orleans voters until voters return or are permanently resettled)

- Promote and expand quality public health care
  —Federally funded health coverage for all hurricane survivors

- Restore public education
  —Immediate access to all public school facilities

- Promote human and community-based economic development
  —Immediate restoration of all public utilities to all neighborhoods of New Orleans

- Community-based economic development and global competitiveness
  —Reject "free enterprise zones," "empowerment zones" and subsidies to large corporations

- Support New Orleans' Indigenous and community artists and culture
  —Pay a living wage to artists, including ensemble members like Mardi Gras Indians

- Support the rights of all workers and survivors to construction jobs
  —Guarantee full employment at a living wage to all returnees
  —End city support for ICE raids on workplaces and living spaces of reconstruction laborers

- Uphold and advance environmental justice
  —Demand that EPA and DEX remove or remediate sediment on streets, sidewalks, and yards in neighborhoods inundated by toxic floodwaters

- Safeguard the levees and waterway systems
  —Demand Army Corps of Engineers build Category 5 levees immediately, starting with the areas most vulnerable to disaster

Waiting on the Levees

The mayoral elections are over. The city is a shell of its former self. More than half the city is still uninhabitable due to ecological devastation and government corruption, inaction, and racism. In the midst of this, the levees have not been fully repaired, the hurricane season is coming again, and global warming will not be pacified by reactionary evasions or liberal hopes.

As a short-term fix, the Army Corps of Engineers has generated an accelerated $800 million levee repair, even taking the extreme measures of asking the contractor, Granite Construction, to actually finish the job on time or lose the contract. The negatives however are quite severe.

First, while much of the levee system has been repaired and even improved, it is still based on building to "pre-Katrina levels" which at the time, was built to protect against a hurricane with wind speeds of what is now considered a Category 2 storm, or up to 110 miles per hour.

Second, the rapid repair process has been heavily criticized by independent hurricane experts. As the *New York Times* reported:

> The degree of vulnerability was underscored by an independent team of researchers led by engineering professors at the University of California, Berkeley, and

> supported by the National Science Foundation. They released a report that found the hurricane protection system riddled with errors in design, construction, and maintenance—a pattern of inattention to safety that caused the system to crumble in a hurricane that should have, for the most part, caused little more than wind damage and a day or so of street flooding. "The overall New Orleans flood protection system," engineering Professor Seed said, "must be considered suspect."[100]

According to the report, "people died because mistakes were made and because safety was exchanged for efficiency and reduced cost." While the report indicated that some of the new retrofitted work is an improvement, "the parts of the system with sheet piles that were too short before the storm and which are built on weak soil are still very much at risk in a future storm. Under similar circumstances, professor Seed said, "It still will be a very dangerous system."[101]

The People's Hurricane Relief Fund has initiated a new campaign: "The Levee Call: A Life and Death Issue."[102] It focuses national attention on the inadequacies of the levee system, calls for an end to the war in Iraq as a competing and degraded national priority, and asserts, "given the consequences of global warming and the woefully inadequate investment in levee repair since Katrina, levee repair remains a matter of life and death."

The call proposes a strategic alliance of progressive groups, constituencies, and causes.

> We invite both the massive movement in the Mexican, Latino, and Asian communities demanding immigrant rights,

> and the anti-war movement to link with a movement for Reconstruction and the Right of Return to the Gulf Coast. We are all challenging the same system of oppression. And there is a developing recognition that our unity would represent a powerful force for human rights and global justice—a force not seen since the massive mobilizations of the 1960s.
>
> Reconstruction in the Gulf Coast forces the U.S. to choose between financing wars abroad and providing for the life and death needs of an African American majority that it claims are "full American citizens" no longer oppressed by a racist economic and political system. The government's abandonment of the people of the Gulf Coast graphically exposes the racist U.S. war at home and discredits its claim to being a democratic country.
>
> This movement is no longer about "relief." A United Front for building levees takes the initiative to challenge the system that thrives on death, ethnic cleansing, gentrification, and denial of all peoples' human rights.

The call has many creative demands and tactical plans. Of particular importance is its proposal to "Link with the Latino movement—connecting the need for a levee system as walls for life, with opposition to the construction of the 700 mile long wall of death along the U.S. Mexico border."[103]

The Ecological Future of New Orleans: Can the Movement Imagine a Revolutionary Relocation Plan?

There is a legitimate debate about the long-term viability of New Orleans as a city below sea level, and abstract, if still relevant, proposals in the incubation stage, about rebuilding the city in a safer, more ecologically stable location. Given the widespread denial of the true consequences of global warming even among progressive and left organizers and community residents, this issue should be put on the table. It should not, however, become the property of the careerist interventions of architects and urban planners who are too often in sharp contradiction to social movements and reflect the interests of downtown developers.

All ideas, however, must be situated in time, place, and conditions. Right now, meaning for the next decade after Katrina, the first step is to rebuild New Orleans within its present geographical limits, in a way to protect the city and rebuild the levees as well as possible in the wake of the inevitable future hurricanes, perhaps of enormous proportions. The most important step is to rebuild the areas of New Orleans, such as the Lower Ninth ward, with a massive infusion of funds, and to facilitate the repatriation of hundreds of thousands Black residents. The immediate architectural and urban planning challenge is how to raise the level of some of the lower areas of the city, how to replace soft substrate with more durable materials, how to create a multi-billion dollar makeover for the urban poor, and how to create a state of the art levee system, as exists in the Netherlands. Then, with the city back to its racial and cultural whole, a revolutionary vision in itself, the entire community, Black, Latino, Asian, and white, can have an informed discussion of its future, including the option to move the entire city further away from the sea line, and onto drier and higher ground. It is urgent that visionary organizers in New Orleans visit representatives of the Small Island States, and visit islands such as Tuvalu,

Samoa, and the Marshall Islands, to see first hand the devastating impacts of global warming on other below-sea level societies. Many Pacific Islanders are demanding the right to relocate with full rights to Western, more stable inland areas—such as Australia, and so far, not surprisingly, have been denied by the illegitimate residents of that white settler state. One definition of "visionary" is the capacity of a leader to see ahead into uncharted areas, and to bring new ideas to oppressed people that they can integrate and develop as their own. The long-term future of many coastal cities throughout the world is not viable unless there is a true revolution of culture, economics, production, and consumption that literally turns the internal combustion engine and the auto based culture on its head. For if the ravages of global warming are not reversed, even the most progressive, pro-Black administration and movement in New Orleans and many areas of the Gulf Coast will not be able to hold back the long-term ravages of our fossil-fuel created Armageddon.

Still, a revolutionary vision must combine an expansive view of the future with a profound grasp of the present. Right now, the last thing Black people in the New Orleans Diaspora want to focus on is a new location for the city. For them, they are already in a new location—and one not of their own choosing. Their ties to this historically Black city, its historically Black majority, Black culture, and Black institutions are the driving force in their lives. If we lived in an antiracist, socialist oriented, political democracy with strong environmental policies, unwavering protections for historically oppressed nationalities, and a strong Black Left, we could consider a national policy of rebuilding a network of coastal cities in a way that could be in the best interests of New Orleans' Black majority and the society as a whole. However, we presently live in a on-the-way-to-fascist society with racism as national policy—a society invading Iraq and threatening to do the same to Iran, intent upon overthrowing the progressive Chavez regime in Venezuela, a society in the grips of a fraudulent and permanent war against terrorism of which the U.S. is the primary culprit. At a time when the levees are being built on the cheap, and the Black Diaspora is crying to return home, it smacks of the worst white liberal privilege and arrogance to "imagine" the future of a Black city without the Black residents in it.

The Movement Begins with What We Have

In 1989, after the fall of the Soviet Union and the Berlin Wall, there was a widespread perception that the movement of the world Left had come to an end. Many bought into Margaret Thatcher's assertion of capitalism's inevitability: "There is no alternative." After the events of September 11, 2001 and the brilliant right-wing exploitation of the crisis of its own making, many progressive people felt, with good reason, that George Bush and his thugs would have a lifetime franchise to impose the military state and white supremacy at home and abroad.

Today, five years after September 11, the wheels are falling off the Bush bandwagon. Public opposition is coming from across the political spectrum, not at all limited to liberals and the Left. The war in Iraq is a political and military disaster and is strengthening international forces that see the U.S. bogged down in a quagmire. The government's catastrophic modeling of cynicism and incompetence in the face of Katrina is seen as quintessential racism as national policy—even in the eyes of many white people. Even some conservative Republicans have grave concerns about U.S. torture of prisoners and assassination of civilians in Iraq, its spying on the library books and emails of U.S. residents, its leaking of the identities of CIA agents who disagree with its policies, and the president's and Cheney's views of executive privilege that extend to FBI invasions of congresspeople's offices.

The once unbeatable Bush is now a lame-duck, if still powerful, president. His approval rating, below 38 percent of eligible voters, has fallen like a bag of rocks. But Bush is a crusader, a man on a mission. He understands that he has won two terms to carry out his extreme right-wing agenda, and unlike the disgraceful Democrats, he does not really care too much about his "poll numbers." The war on Iraq goes on, the police state ratchets up, a militarized border patrol is proposed against Mexico and Mexicans, the U.S. sends extra missiles to Israel to rain down on Lebanese civilians, and Bush does not plan to do anything to help New Orleans's dispersed 250,000 Black refugees. Bush understands the importance of state power and will not take one step back until his term is over, after which he will actively campaign for an ideologically compatible successor. We on the Left have to find the forms of organization and the ideological will to fight a war to the death to take on the Right. Such a war will have to go far beyond facile critiques, the network of self-important and ineffective internet lieutenants, and the hope that the Right will fall of its own weight—some of the many opiates of the Left.

Sadly, but predictably, the opportunity created by Bush's over-extending his electoral mandate, and the inchoate but substantial opposition to the Bush-Cheney neo-fascist takeover is being sabotaged and misdirected by the Democratic Party. The Democratic Party elite is suppressing the best intentions of its own voters and even the delegates to its own presidential nominating convention who are generally for civil rights and an immediate withdrawal from Iraq. The Democratic Leadership Council has imposed a dictatorship over most of the Democratic Party, and is implementing an unethical, cowardly, and self-defeating tactical plan: "say nothing, allow public opposition the Bush to grow, and hope we win by default in 2006 and 2008." Their only hope: a "No" vote on Bush. Their thinking: "The polls indicate that if we fight for Blacks and Latinos, against the national security state, against the war, and if we fight for social security by launching a coherent support of the social welfare state we may lose the long-sought-after Reagan/Bush Republicans and the vaunted soccer moms and NASCAR dads, a.k.a. white southern, midwestern, suburban, Christian, conservative folks." Thus, at a time when we urgently need a broad liberal, progressive, left united front, the Democratic Party, and even its once progressive wing, has no intention of being part of one.

As during the 1960s, there are nascent, small, antiracist, anti-imperialist social movements developing in opposition to both the Democrats and Republicans, as young people on campuses and in low-income communities of color have begun to look at the system itself for the causes of September 11. They see the "war on terrorism" as a perpetual, aggressive, and unprovoked "war against the world," including domestic dissent in the U.S. They are sick of the Democrats, see through John Kerry and Hillary Clinton, and want in some way to build an independent grassroots Left. But how? The fusion between these nascent movements, including the few left-wing and reform Democrats, and the New Orleans and Gulf Coast resistance would be a significant step forward for a hoped-for and not-yet-realized mass antiracist Left. Those movements and forces of resistance are still modest in scope, but we should be thankful they exist, for they are the building blocks of any future hope.

Almost a year after Katrina, the New Orleans and Gulf Coast situation continues to present a massive and ongoing crisis for the U.S. political system. There is great opportunity to educate broad sections of the U.S. population, especially in the Black, Latino, Asian/Pacific Islander, and Indigenous communities, with a primary focus on the working classes of those communities, and from there, to reach out to the relative large base of liberal, progressive, and left white constituencies about the crisis of the imperialist system under which we live—and the need for the most radical, structural solutions.

The future is always fought out in the present—from a mayoral election to a fight to save one house or a thousand homes in the Lower Ninth Ward to the demands for a massive strengthening of the Voting Rights Act to the critical nation-building demands of the Right of Return and the right to safe levees before the next disaster.

Today, the movement is still having great difficulty finding its own voice. It cannot break out of its self-imposed shackles. It is not yet at the stage of a great idea in embryo, or close to an organizational breakthrough in which key organizers reach a level of historical agreement. No one group or groups has been able to come up with a post-Soviet, post-capitalist China analysis of the world situation, and put forth a coherent ideological alternative. The anti-imperialist Left is weak and divided—many groups and individuals do not even like each other, and we have not yet established a united front culture and process of effective struggle and negotiation in which disagreements and antagonisms can be effectively resolved in the interest of a greater strategic goal. Most work has become local with many unresolved disagreements and conflicts within each oppressed nationality group and between oppressed nationality groups and antiracist and progressive whites. The white liberals have abandoned any commitment to or concern about the inner cities, and are obsessed with saving the sinking ship of the Democratic Party. They represent no independent base, no social movement to compare to the vitality of the Right, and unlike the Right, who keep pushing the Republicans on gun control, gay marriage, escalation of hostility to immigrants, the liberals make no demands on the Democrats except, "here is my money, please try to defeat Bush." For them, campaign finance reform or electing a new Congressman from Idaho is more compelling than addressing the system's racism that perpetuates the crisis of New Orleans.

In the U.S., the rebuilding process will take decades and cannot simply be wished into existence. During the 1930s, it was the Communist Party USA that attracted the best and the brightest and most dedicated cadre. It had a coherent strategy (marred by disastrous decisions on political line impacted by Soviet and Comintern policies), an excellent organization, and a capacity to generate broad united fronts inside the Congress of Industrial Organizations (CIO), the Black civil rights movement, veterans, "foreign born," international support for the Spanish Civil War, and the fight against evictions. It generated a multi-tiered and coherent set of publications—*Daily World, New Masses*—and attracted great support from left intellectuals throughout the world. It's support, if only temporary, for the concept of a Black nation in the South and its courageous antiracist work led many to call it "the Party of the Negro." The CPUSA was a constructive force in a broad anti-fascist united front that led to the defeat of Hitler and the Axis powers.

During the world-wide "Slave Revolts" of the 1950s-1970s, a new Left, lead by oppressed nationality peoples and antiracist whites, carried out a broad strategy of an antiracist, anti-imperialist united front, and worked from a more multi-tendency model. The Second Reconstruction generated impressive organizations—the Student Non-Violent Coordinating Committee, Students for a Democratic Society, La Raza Unida Party and the Brown Berets, U.S. China People's Friendship Association, the Venceremos Brigades, the Red Guards, a network of women's collectives, and the "party-building" Marxist-Leninist groups that arose from those histories. Again, as during the 1930s, the movement attracted a group of passionate intellectuals who saw themselves in service to the more militant and committed front line organizations, and generated a panoply of newspapers, theater groups, and experiments in armed propaganda. The broad united front of the Second Reconstruction was able to defeat formal apartheid and Jim Crow segregation, helped to strengthen the women's, gay and lesbian, environmental movements, and was part of a successful worldwide movement to defeat the United States invasion of Vietnam and to allow the Vietnamese people independence and self-determination.

The leadership of the Communist Party USA and the 1930s Left, and, later, the revolutionary Left of the Second Reconstruction were badly injured by a pattern of massive governmental suppression—from the McCarthy period to the later COINTELPRO interventions by the CIA, FBI, U.S. Congress, local police, and the corporate media. Today, through the Homeland Security apparatus, a right-wing noose has already been placed around the neck of a new, if unsuspeccting, movement. It is only the relative weakness and disorientation of today's movement and the relatively few efforts to militantly exercise its civil rights and civil liberties that prevents us from comprehending the full scale and impact of the already constructed police state poised to repress domestic dissent.

In this context, the larger U.S. movement needs to nurture any forms of resistance in New Orleans and the Gulf Coast—to provide lawyers and doctors, visiting organizers able to work effectively and under the leadership of Black-led groups in the impacted areas, to pressure members of

Congress and campaigns of support for new levees and new resettlement campaigns in New Orleans. The movement for a Black Reconstruction is in constant need of funding for its work. Movement aid for movement groups continues to be the operative principle to help build a national support network to encourage funding the broadest possible united front in New Orleans and the Gulf Coast.

The movement cannot advance by imagining new groups, new politics that do not exist outside the actual class struggle. The future strengthening of the movement will come out of those who are on the ground confronting the enemy and the empire, navigating principled disagreements that arise out of practice. There is an urgent need for grassroots leaders with the most mature, united front building skills, as some of the absurd conflicts among groups on the ground in New Orleans are taking on tragic proportions. This can allow groups to carry out their tactical plans with a level of independence and initiative while working energetically to model how a united front can be built in spite of personal, racial, and strategic tensions.

A Third Black Reconstruction could ally with forces in the Third World, learn from their resiliency in fighting even more brutal forms of repression and dictatorship exercised by the U.S. government, raise concrete demands that place the burden on the system, and challenge the reaction and treachery of both major parties.

A Third Black Reconstruction could expand the fight for democratic rights into a conscious united front against racism, imperialism, and fascism. The U.S. ruling class has made the conscious assessment that as it works to dismantle what is left of the welfare state, pushes wages and benefits down, allows corporations to file bankruptcy to cancel pension plans, works to gut social security, locks up more than 2 million people in prison, and tries to usher in a new concept of permanent war against "terrorism" (for when could it ever end with that definition?), it will require a greater use of state power and repression against every element of a possible domestic resistance. In this context, a U.S. Left if it looks squarely in the mirror, confronts it own weaknesses with an uncompromising eye, and "claims no easy victories," can help lead a broad democratic front against racism, war, empire, and fascism. That is not just a hypothetical opportunity; it has become the most clear and effective strategy and the only way out for all progressive people in the U.S.

The latest disclosures of the crimes and punishments of the Bush Administration create a critical opportunity for the movement in New Orleans and the Gulf Coast to push its most structural, militant demands. We know the movement in every city is not as strong or unified as we would like, but these historical crises are cracks in the ruling class levees, splits that will create new tactical options and opportunities.

The present crisis of the system—from Iraq to New Orleans, from the police to the prisons, and from the disintegration of the welfare state to the disintegration of the society as a whole—offers a great opportunity to advance a new stage of the Black Liberation Movement, a new stage in the building of a broad non-sectarian Left, a chance to weaken the stranglehold of the two-party Right. That is the ongoing challenge to all of us, to find ways to offer the most effective aid to the embattled and courageous Black people of New Orleans and the Gulf Coast, and to transfer outrage into the most structural, and concrete demands on the system. As our African comrades say, *La Lutta Continua*—the struggle continues.

Notes

1. I have been using the concept of the "two decades of the sixties" for several years to describe the actual scope of the last period of Left influence in U.S. life—what I have also referred to as the Second Reconstruction. Many of the young organizers in today's movement were not even born during that period, or were small children at the time—and thus depend upon historians to reconstruct the record. Part of the present "Age of Reaction" has included the rewriting of the great achievements of revolutionary history reflected in popular caricatures and slanders of the revolutionary Left of that period, from right-wing and liberal critics to some disillusioned, recanting former revolutionaries. Thus, in many sources, "the sixties" has become an ossified and undialectical period, as if the 1950s were conservative, the 1960s radical, the 1970s moderate and the 1980s conservative, (and to continue this analogy, the 1990s and 2000s reactionary). In actuality, the seeds of the revolutionary period began in the heart of the right-wing, Cold War, racist, McCarthyite fifties. The "two decades of the sixties" began with the 1954 *Brown v. Board of Education* decision, the 1955 Montgomery Bus Boycott, and the historic 1955 Bandung (Indonesia) Conference of Non-Aligned Nations (challenging the hegemony of the United States). This period did not end clearly until the election of Reagan in 1980, but the high point at the end of this period was 1975, when the last U.S. soldiers were evacuated from Vietnam, the U.S.-supported south Vietnamese government fell, and shortly thereafter, the colonial city of Saigon was renamed Ho Chi Minh city, by the victorious troops of the National Liberation Front of Vietnam.
2. Saladin Muhammad, "Hurricane Katrina: The Black Nation's 9/11!" Synthesis/Regeneration 39 (Winter 2006).
3. W.E.B. Du Bois, *Black Reconstruction in America* (New York: The Free Press, 1962), p. 30.
4. Ibid., p. 149, Du Bois cites Lincoln from Charles Wesley, "Lincoln's Plan for Colonizing the Emancipated Negro," *Journal of Negro History* IV (20).
5. George Breitman, ed., *Malcolm X Speaks* (New York: Grove Press, 1990).
6. Du Bois, *Black Reconstruction, op. cit.*
7. W.E.B. Du Bois, "The Freedmen's Bureau," Atlantic Monthly 87 (1901), p. 354.
8. Komozi Woodard, *A Nation within a Nation: Amiri Baraka and Black Power Politics* (Chapel Hill: University of North Carolina Press, 1999), p. 20.

9. Charles Sumner, speech as a U.S. congressmember, at the impeachment trial of President Andrew Johnson, 30th March, 1868, http://www.spartacus.schoolnet.co.uk/USASsumner.htm.

10. "Minutes of an interview between the colored ministers and church officers at Savannah with the Secretary of War and Major-General Sherman," Headquarters of Major-General Sherman, City of Savannah, GA, Thursday, January 12, 1865. Published in *A Documentary History of Emancipation, 1861-1867*, ed. Ira Berlin, et al., Volume 3, Series 1: *The Wartime Genesis of Free Labor: The Lower South* (Port Chester: Cambridge University Press, 1991), pp. 331-38.

11. Ibid., pp. 338-40.

12. Benjamin Wade, letter to Uriah Painter of the *New York Times*, 1867, http://www.spartacus.schoolnet.co.uk/USASradical.htm.

13. Amiri Baraka, *The Leroi Jones/Amiri Baraka Reader* (New York: Thunder's Mouth Press, 1999), pp. 555-556.

14. Mao-Tse-tung, *Analysis of the Classes in Chinese Society, Mao-Tse-tung Collected Works* (Peking: Foreign Languages Press, 1967).

15. "From 1964 to 1971, there were more than 750 riots, killing 228 people and injuring 12,741 others. After more than 15,000 separate incidents of arson, many black urban neighborhoods were in ruins." Virginia Postrel, "The Consequences of the 1960's Race Riots Come Into View," *New York Times*, December 20, 2004.

16. As Strategy Center researcher Palak Shah explained, "There is wide variance in how many rebellions occurred during the 1960s, mostly because researchers have focused on cities with large Black populations, newspaper reports only, and/or excluded uprisings in schools and smaller cities." A study led by sociology professor Daniel Meyers that analyzed this bias located 1,357 "riot" events. He claims that even the most complete studies contain only 752 events and this is over an 8-year period (1964-1971). According to his tabulation, 458 cities experienced at least one rebellion from 1967-1969. Dr. Daniel Meyers, "Racial Riots in the United States, 1967-1972," University of Notre Dame, http://www.nd.edu/~dmyers/team/frp.html.

17. Eric Mann, "Newark—It Was Like a Happening," *The Movement*, newsletter of SNCC, 3:8, 1967. Author's note: I was living in the Black community (South Ward) in Newark, New Jersey during the urban rebellion. From my apartment, surrounded by national guard troops that killed 23 people and injured 725, I wrote this article for a predominantly white audience, trying to explain to white liberals why Black people would rebel and why white people should support such urban rebellions.

18 Jessie Carney Smith, "First National Black Political Convention Held..." Published in *Black Firsts: 2,000 Years of Extraordinary Achievement*, (Detroit: Visible Ink Press, 1994).

19. "Black Panther Party Platform and Program." African American Historical Documents available at: http://www.africanamericans.com/BlackPantherPartyPlatform.html.

20. Willie Horton was a Black prisoner, incarcerated in Concord State Prison for first degree murder, who was released under a weekend furlough program in 1986, under a program established by the Massachusetts legislature and supported by then Massachusetts Governor Michael Dukakis. Horton never came back to prison, and while out on the streets, he viciously attacked a couple—stabbing the man and raping the woman. During the 1988 presidential election, George Bush, Sr. ran pictures of Horton and charged "liberal" Dukakis with allowing [Black] men to roam the streets committing crimes. Bush's campaign manager, Lee Atwater (a clone of Karl Rove), bragged that "before this election is over, Willie Horton will become a household name." It is widely agreed that the "Horton" incident scared the hell out of white voters and was a major factor in Dukakis' defeat and Bush's election.

21. Joan Parkin, "Throwing Away the Key: The World's Leading Jailer," *International Socialist Review* 21 (Jan-Feb 2002), p. 69

22. Terrence Hunt and Nedra Pickler, "Bush: New Orleans 'will rise again,'" *Chicago Tribune*, September 15, 2005.

23. Congressional Black Caucus, 109th Congress, "H.R. 4197—Hurricane Katrina Recovery, Reclamation, Restoration, Reconstruction, and Reunion Act of 2005," November 2, 2005.

24. Glen Ford and Peter Gamble, "Katrina: Shock Therapy for Black America," *Black Commentator*, February 23, 2006, http://www.blackcommentator.com/172/172_cover_katrina_shock.html.

25 Reverend Lennox Yearwood, interview by Eric Mann and Damon Azali, *Voices from the Front Lines*, KPFK 90.7 FM, Los Angeles, February 2, 2006.

26. *U.S. Constitution*, Article 1 Section 2, Clause 3.

27. Randall Robinson, *The Debt: What America Owes to Blacks* (New York: Dutton, 2000).

28. Communist International, "Resolutions on the Afro-American National Question, 1928 and 1930."

29. Bob Wing, "White Power in Election 2000," *Colorlines*, Spring 2001.

30. Robinson, *op. cit.*
31. Robinson, *The Debt*, p. 231.
32. Robert Westley, "Many Billions Gone," *Boston College Law Review*, June 1999.
33. Robinson, *The Debt*, pp. 244-245.
34. See Eric Mann, *Dispatches from Durban: Firsthand Commentaries on the World Conference Against Racism and Post September 11 Movement Strategies* (Los Angeles: Front Lines Press, 2002).
35. Saladin Muhammad, interview with the author, September 26, 2005. See also Eric Mann, *Dispatches from Durban.*
36. A beautiful, if heartbreaking film that documents these crimes against Black farmers is *Homecoming: The Story of African American Farmers*, available at www.pbs.org. The figures cited are from the PBS companion website to the film, http://www.pbs.org/itvs/homecoming/resources.html. See also Anuradha Mittal and Joan Powell, "The Last Plantation Backgrounder," Food First/Institute for Food and Development Policy, Winter 2000.
37. Congressman William Lacy Clay, Floor Statement of Congressman Clay on Black Land Loss, February 7, 2002, http://www.house.gov/clay/pr020207.htm.
38. Beverly Wright, interview by Eric Mann and Damon Azali, *Voices from the Frontlines*, KPFK 90.7 FM, Los Angeles, September 16, 2005.
39. David Streitfeld, "Speculators Rushing in as the Water Recedes," *Los Angeles Times*, September 15, 2005.
40. Eric Mann, et al, *Reconstructing Los Angeles, and U.S. Cities, from the Bottom Up* (Los Angeles: Labor/Community Strategy Center, 1993).
41. *African Americans and Climate Change: An Unequal Burden*, Congressional Black Caucus Foundation, July 21, 2004. (Thanks to Ansje Miller of Redefining Progress for her help.)
42. Hurricane News, "Sustaining Category Five Intensity," http://www.hurricaneville.com/catfiveintensity.html, (accessed 2/3/06).
43. *Rising Waters: Global Warming and the Fate of the Pacific Islands*, VHS, produced by Andrea Torrice (Oley, PA: Bullfrog Films, 2000).
44. Ronald Brownstein, "Hard Choices Blow in the Winds of Katrina, and Now Rita," *Los Angeles Times*, September 26, 2005.
45. Enele Sopoaga, interview by Amy Goodman, *Democracy Now!*, December 28, 2004.

46. Paul R. Epstein, "Is Global Warming Harmful to Health?" *Scientific American*, August 2000.

47. Brian Azcona and Jason Neville, "Unnatural Disaster: Louisiana's Crisis in Policy and Planning," September 4, 2005. The authors can be reached at: blazcona@ku.edu and jason.neville@usc.edu. (Thanks to Ted Glick of the Climate Crisis Coalition for forwarding this paper.)

48. Ibid.

49. Institute for Women's Policy Research, "Women of Gulf Coast Key to Rebuilding After Katrina and Rita," October 11, 2005, 1, http://www.iwpr.org/pdf/NewOrleans_Part1.pdf. Based on report, *The Women of New Orleans and the Gulf Coast: Multiple Disadvantages and Key Assets for Recovery: Part I. Poverty, Race, Gender and Class*, Barbara Gault, Heidi Hartmann, Avis Jones-DeWeever, Misha Werschkul, and Erica Williams. Available at http://www.iwpr.org/pdf/D464.pdf.

50. Ibid., p. 3.

51. Joni Seager, "Natural Disasters Expose Gender Divides," *Chicago Tribune*, September 14, 2005.

52. Ibid.

53. Ibid.

54. Loretta J. Ross, "A Feminist Perspective on Katrina," *Collective Voices*, Issue 3, September 11, 2005.

55. Ibid., p. 1.

56. Ibid., p. 3.

57. Ibid., pp. 3-4.

58. Reuters, "LA Governor Warns Troops Will 'Shoot and Kill'," *Yahoo! News*, September 2, 2005.

59. For an excellent analysis of the rise and fall of grassroots movements, see *Poor People's Movements: Why They Succeed, How They Fail*, by Frances Fox Piven and Richard A. Cloward, (New York; Random House, 1977) and the 1966 film *Troublemakers*, by Norman Fruchter and Robert Machover, which chronicled the organizing of the Newark Community Union Project.

60. Mann, *Reconstructing Los Angeles, op. cit.*

61. Eric Mann et. al., *A Call to Reject the Federal Weed and Seed Program in Los Angeles* (Los Angeles: Labor/Community Strategy Center, 1992).

62. Mann, *Reconstructing Los Angeles, op. cit.*

63. Mike Davis, "Who is Killing New Orleans?" *The Nation*, April 10, 2006, p. 14.

64. Ibid.

65a. *The Bureau of Justice Statistics Bulletin: Prison and Jail Inmates at Midyear 2005*, U.S. Department of Justice, Office of Justice Programs. Revised, 6/5/06. http://www.ojp.usdoj.gov/bjs/pub/pdf/pjim05.pdf.

65b. Rebecca Carroll, "Report: Correctional Supervision Rising," *Associated Press*, November 2, 2005.

66. Human Rights Watch, "Race and Incarceration in the United States," a Human Rights Watch Press Backgrounder, February 27, 2002.

67. Ibid.

68. Uriah J. Fields, "Katrina and Race," Authorsden.com, September 06, 2005.

69. Human Rights Watch, "New Orleans: Prisoners Abandoned to Floodwaters," *Human Rights News*, September 22, 2005.

70. Editoral, "Trapped in a Flooding Jail Cell," *New York Times*, September 29, 2005.

71. "There's a Better Way to Make our Streets Safe," Safe Streets/Strong Communities, which can be reached at 504-522-3949 x250, New Orleans, LA.

72. The August Twenty-Ninth Movement (ML), "Fan the Flames: A Revolutionary Position of the Chicano National Question," (1975-76), p. 10.

73. Bill Fletcher, visiting professor, Political Science, Brooklyn College, conversation with the author, April 25, 2006.

74. Glen Ford, "The Insanity of Black Anti-Immigrant Politics," *The Black Commentator*, Issue 177, March 30, 2006.

75. Saladin Muhammad, "African Americans and Latinos Unite: Build a United Democratic Front," talk to Workers World Party, May 15, 2006.

76. Gregory Rodriguez, "La Nueva Orleans," *Los Angeles Times*, September 25, 2005.

77. Kelly Brewington, "New Orleans Rebuilds as Tensions Rise," *Baltimore Sun*, October 14, 2005.

78. "Taking it to the Streets," *Los Angeles Times*, May 2, 2006.

79. Eric Mann, Lisa Duran, Bill Gallegos, and Glen Omatsu (primary authors), *Immigrant Rights and Wrongs* (Los Angeles: Labor/Community Strategy Center, Urban Strategies Group, 1994).

80. C. Stone Browne, "Katrina's Forgotten Victims: Native American Tribes," *Pacific News Service*, September 11, 2005.

81. For a discussion of the under-reported developments in the Gulf Coast Vietnamese community, see Eric Tang, "Boat People: the precarious position of the Vietnamese from the Gulf Coast," *Colorlines Magazine*, Spring, 2006.

82. Congresswoman Diane Watson to Congressman Dennis Hastert, September 1, 2005, http://www.house.gov/apps/list/press/ca333_watson/050901.html.

83. "Poll: Fewer than Half Think U.S. Will Win in Iraq," *CNN.com*, September 22, 2005, http://www.cnn.com/2005/POLITICS/09/22/iraq.poll/.

84. U.S. Senator Barack Obama, Address to Chicago Council on Foreign Relations, November 22, 2005, http://obama.senate.gov/speech/051122-moving_forward_in_iraq/index.html.

85. Statement of Congressional Hispanic Caucus, "Hispanic Caucus Urges Bush Administration to Accept Cuban Offer of Doctors for Hurricane Relief," September 8, 2005. All 21 members of the Caucus endorsed the statement.

86. "Venezuela Offers Fuel, Food, to Hurricane Hit-US," *Agence France-Presse*, August 29, 2005.

87. William L. Patterson , editor, *We Charge Genocide: The Crime of Government Against the Negro People*, International Publishers. 2001. ISBN 0717803120. "We Charge Genocide" was a document presented to the United Nations in 1951 by William L. Patterson of the Civil Rights Congress, arguing that the U.S. federal government, by its failure to act against lynching in the United States, was guilty of genocide under Article II of the UN Genocide Convention.

88. Muhammad, *op. cit.*

89. Jason DeParle, "Liberal Hopes Ebb in Post-Storm Poverty Debate: An Ideological Clash Over How to Help America's Poor," *New York Times*, October 11, 2005.

90. Lewis Reine, Secretary Treasurer of the Lousiana AFL-CIO, interview by Eric Mann, co-host, on a joint KPFK 90.7 FM, Los Angeles and KPFA 94.1 FM, Berkeley statewide broadcast on the statewide initiatives facing the electorate, October 29, 2005.

91. Dr. Robert Bullard, interview with the author, September 8, 2005.

92. Curtis Muhammad, talk at Labor/Community Strategy Center Evening in Solidarity with the New Orleans & Gulf Coast Movements of Resistance, Los Angeles, California, October 6, 2005.

93. Robert Tanner, "As New Orleans Rebuilds, Will Poor be Cut Out?", Associated Press story, *Houston Chronicle*, October 12, 2005.

94. Harry Belafonte, statement during the National Townhall Meeting at the 35th Annual Legislative Conference of the Congressional Black Caucus,

September 21, 2005. A webcast can be found at the Congressional Black Caucus Foundation webpage, http://www.broadcasturban.net/webcast/cbcf2005/thu_townhall.htm. The conference was attended by Damon Azali and Barbara Lott-Holland of the Labor/Community Strategy Center.

95. Eric Mann, *The 2004 Elections—a Challenge to the U.S. Left* (Los Angeles: Progressives and Independents to Defeat Bush,, 2004).

96. Blaine Harden, "The Changing Face of New Orleans: Wealth, Race, Guiding Which Residents Stay and which Never Return," *Washington Post*, May 17, 2006.

97. "Landrieu endorsed by Morton and other members of local clergy," *Louisiana Weekly*, May 8, 2006.

98. Katrina Information Network media alert, June 1, 2006, "More Hurricanes Coming: As Services Decrease Katrina's Displaced form Survivor's Councils and Get Organized," www.katrinainfonet.net.

99. Ibid.

100. John Schwartz, "Levees Rebuilt Just in Time, but Doubts Remain," *New York Times,* May 25, 2006.

101. Ibid.

102. People's Hurricane Relief Fund and Oversight Committee, Kali Akuno and Saladin Muhammad, campaign coordinators, "The Levee Call: A Life and Death Issue" May 27, 2006.

103. Ibid.

Index

About the Author

Eric Mann is director of the Labor/Community Strategy Center and member of the Bus Riders Union Planning Committee in Los Angeles. He has been a civil rights, anti-Vietnam war, labor, and environmental organizer with the Congress of Racial Equality, Students for a Democratic Society, and the United Auto Workers, including eight years on auto assembly lines. In 2001 he was a delegate to the U.N. World Conference Against Racism in Durban, South Africa where he participated in the protests against the U.S. government's walk out. He returned to South Africa in 2002 as part of a Strategy Center delegatation to the World Summit on Sustainable Development in Johannesburg. He is the co-host of the weekly radio show, *Voices from the Frontlines*, on KPFK Pacifica in Los Angeles.

Books by Eric Mann

Comrade George: *An Investigation into the Life, Political Thought, and Assassination of George Jackson*

"*Comrade George* is a passionate, yet, careful, analysis of the life and assassination of George Jackson. Its language is angry, but it subjects the official explanation of Jackson's death to a meticulous examination. More important, it connects the killings of Jackson to the current upsurge of revolt in the prisons. One cannot read this book without a feeling of outrage at the inhumanity of the system we live under. And yet, one also comes away with a sense of the possibilities that an ongoing struggle possesses for the future."

—Howard Zinn

Taking on General Motors: *A Case Study of the UAW Campaign to Keep GM Van Nuys Open*

"I have marched with the Van Nuys UAW workers and observed their masterful organizing work first-hand. This complex case study of the construction of a successful labor/community movement to save L.A.'s last auto plant should be savored. If you are a labor or civil rights organizer, an environmental or peace activist, a college or high school teacher, or a member of the Rainbow Coalition, I urge you to read and distribute *Taking On General Motors* and creatively apply its many lessons to your own work."

—Rev. Jesse Jackson

L.A.'s Lethal Air: *New Strategies for Policy, Organizing, and Action*

"*L.A.'s Lethal Air* is a breath of fresh air; it translates cold environment statistics into a story about people. The chapter on 'Class, Race, and Gender: The Unspoken Categories of Public Health' is a major breakthrough in environmental analysis. *L.A.'s Lethal Air* makes a unique, well-documented contribution to the environmental movement by placing responsibility for the devastating public health impacts of air pollution clearly at the feet of corporate America—and generating positive grassroots proposals for industrial and transportation policy."

—Barry Commoner

DISPATCHES FROM DURBAN: *Firsthand Commentaries on the World Conference Against Racism and Post-September 11 Movement Strategies*

"Eric Mann, a major voice on the Left for nearly four decades, takes the U.S. Left on an international journey. He imagines a Left capable of blocking U.S. intervention in Third World countries, battling corporate globalization, and defending the rights of oppressed nationalities here in the 'belly of the beast.' He highlights the Reparations Movement's revolutionary potential to expose the relationship between the development of capitalism, racism, colonialism and slavery, and to strike directly at the World Bank, the IMF, the G8 nations, and the U.S. itself. There is a refreshing, at times startling, realpolitik optimism running throughout this book."

—Robin D. G. Kelley

THE 2004 ELECTIONS: *A Turning Point for the U.S. Left*

"Eric Mann offers us this election year's clearest analysis. Not only of the political forces at work but also of how to move forward and have an effect on the coming election. A refreshing development, that the most complete analysis of our current political situation is coupled with a means for its implementation, and does not remain solely an intellectual exercise."

—Colin Bosio Cody